THE

COPENHAGEN

PAPERS

fiction
SPIES
HEADLONG
THE TIN MEN
THE RUSSIAN INTERPRETER
TOWARDS THE END OF
   THE MORNING
A VERY PRIVATE LIFE
SWEET DREAMS
THE TRICK OF IT
A LANDING ON THE SUN
NOW YOU KNOW

plays
ALARMS & EXCURSIONS
COPENHAGEN
NOW YOU KNOW
HERE
LOOK LOOK
BENEFACTORS
NOISES OFF
MAKE AND BREAK
BALMORAL
CLOUDS
DONKEYS' YEARS
ALPHABETICAL ORDER
THE TWO OF US

translations
UNCLE VANYA (Chekhov)
THREE SISTERS (Chekhov)
THE CHERRY ORCHARD
   (Chekhov)
THE SNEEZE (Chekhov)
WILD HONEY (Chekhov)
THE FRUITS OF
   ENLIGHTENMENT (Tolstoy)
EXCHANGE (Trifonov)
NUMBER ONE (Anouilh)

film and television
CLOCKWISE
FIRST AND LAST
REMEMBER ME?

opera
LA BELLE VIVETTE
   (from Offenbach's
   La Belle Hélène)

THE COPENHAGEN PAPERS

AN INTRIGUE

MICHAEL FRAYN
AND DAVID BURKE

PICADOR

A METROPOLITAN BOOK
HENRY HOLT AND COMPANY
NEW YORK

The authors wish to thank Petra Abendroth
for her contribution to this book.

THE COPENHAGEN PAPERS. Copyright © 2000 by Michael Frayn and David
Burke. All rights reserved. Printed in the United States of America. No part of
this book may be used or reproduced in any manner whatsoever without written permission except in the case of brief quotations embodied in critical articles or reviews. For information, address Picador, 175 Fifth Avenue, New York,
N.Y. 10010.

www.picadorusa.com

Picador® is a U.S. registered trademark and is used by
Henry Holt and Company under license from Pan Books Limited.

For information on Picador Reading Group Guides, as well as ordering,
please contact the Trade Marketing department at St. Martin's Press.
Phone: 1-800-221-7945 extension 763
Fax: 212-677-7456
E-mail: trademarketing@stmartins.com

Library of Congress Cataloging-in-Publication Data

Frayn, Michael.
[Celia's secret]
    The Copenhagen papers : an intrigue / Michael Frayn and David Burke.
        p. cm.
    Originally published: *Celia's secret*. London : Faber and Faber, 2000.
    ISBN 0-312-42124-9
    1. Frayn, Michael Copenhagen. 2. Forgery of manuscripts—England—
History—20th century. 3. Germans—England—Godmanchester—
History. 4. Nuclear weapons—Germany—History. 5. Godmanchester
(England)—Germany—History. 6. Scientists—Germany—Biography.
7. Atomic bomb—Germany—History. 8. Heisenberg, Werner,
1901–1976. 9. Burke, David, 1934–
I. Burke, David, 1934– II. Title.

PR6056.R3 C45 2001
822'.914—dc21   00-051965

First published in Great Britain as *Celia's Secret*
by Faber and Faber Ltd., London

First Picador Edition: January 2003

10 9 8 7 6 5 4 3 2 1

THE
COPENHAGEN
PAPERS

PROLOGUE

Michael Frayn

It was a long war for the original London cast of my play *Copenhagen*. The three of them—David Burke, Sara Kestelman, and Matthew Marsh—played it from May 1998 until August 1999, first in repertory at the National Theatre for nine months, then straight into the West End to do seven performances a week at the Duchess for another six months. It's a play that makes great demands upon its small cast. All three of them are onstage virtually throughout the evening, discovering quantum mechanics and developing nuclear fission, then exploring some of the philosophical darknesses of the human mind.

On the August night that they finally came to the end of their grueling tour of duty, we all went out to dinner afterward to celebrate. They had certainly earned a celebration, but they must have been almost too tired to enjoy it, like exhausted troops returning from the front, and they must have felt that the rest of us there—Michael Codron, who produced the play in the West End, and who was giving us the dinner; Michael Blakemore, who directed the production; and I—could never share what they had been through.

We had been left behind, the staff officers who had sent the troops into battle, then spent the war in safety and idleness many miles behind the front line.

In spite of all this, David Burke and I, at any rate, spent the evening in the most animated conversation. But then he and I had a great deal to talk about, and a second cause for celebration. For us the evening marked the end not just of his stint at the front but of another long trail—and a rather more bewildering one for both of us.

Like me, David is in his mid-sixties, and though we'd never worked together before I had admired him for a long time, from when I first saw him in the original production of Alan Ayckbourn's *Absurd Person Singular* in 1973, to his most recent appearance as Kent in Richard Eyre's fine production of *Lear* at the National—a great arc of career spanning nearly thirty years and the whole range of English theatre, from the funniest of comedies to the most harrowing of tragedies. His performance as the Danish physicist Niels Bohr in my play had been quite remarkable, and his incarnation of Bohr's celebrated combination of percipience and innocence, of toughness and lovability, had moved me deeply. It was not his acting that we were talking about, however, nor, for that matter, the riches of wisdom and experience that we must both have accumulated in the course of our long lives. We were talking about the contents of the large brown envelope on the floor between our two chairs. We were discussing the mysterious batch of papers whose gradual emergence over the previous months had preoccupied us both almost as intensely as the play had.

The subject of *Copenhagen*, I should explain, is itself a mystery—the strange visit that the German physicist Werner

Heisenberg paid to Niels Bohr in Copenhagen in 1941. They were old friends and colleagues, but Denmark was now under German occupation, and Heisenberg had become an enemy. Though he couldn't say it openly to Bohr, he had also become the head of the Nazi government's nuclear program. The two men had a private conversation that ended abruptly and angrily, and their great friendship along with it, but no one has ever been able to reconstruct what they said to each other, or to agree on what Heisenberg's intentions were in making his unwelcome but evidently pressing visit.

The papers in the large brown envelope at our feet related to a later chapter in the story, when Heisenberg, together with all the other German physicists who had been involved in atomic research, was rounded up by the British at the end of the war and secretly interned for six months in Farm Hall, a country house on the outskirts of Godmanchester, in Huntingdonshire. It was another bizarre episode. As Heisenberg had now told Bohr 299 times in the play:

> Our families in Germany are starving, and there are we sitting down each evening to an excellent formal dinner with our charming host, the British officer in charge of us. It's like a pre-war house-party—one of those house-parties in a play, that's cut off from any contact with the outside world, where you know the guests have all been invited for some secret sinister purpose. No one knows we're there—no one in England, no one in Germany, not even our families. But the war's over. What's happening? Perhaps, as in a play, we're going to be quietly murdered, one by one. In

the meanwhile it's all delightfully civilised. I entertain
the party with Beethoven piano sonatas. Major Rittner, our hospitable gaoler, reads Dickens to us, to improve our English. . . .

"Did these things really happen to me?" wonders Heisenberg
in astonishment as he recalls them. They certainly did, because the events at Farm Hall, unlike those in Copenhagen,
are most thoroughly documented. The house had been com-
prehensively bugged by British Intelligence, who made recordings of the German scientists' unguarded conversations
among themselves in order to find out, presumably, how
much they had discovered about building an atomic bomb.
The transcripts of these recordings were kept secret by the
British government until 1992, when they were at last pried
loose by a combined task force of historians and scientists,
and finally published.

The papers in the envelope, however, were something
else again—a completely new source of information about
Farm Hall—and they cast an astonishing new light on the
story. Now that David was free from the distracting pressures
of those seven mighty performances a week, I suggested to
him that we should collaborate to write a brief account of
the documents, and of the way in which they had come to
light, taking turns to explain how each of us had been involved at each separate stage. He agreed.

So here it is, laid out rather like the dialogue in a play.
MF speaks first; DB speaks second; and we shall both have
a lot more to say to each other before we are through. It's
a bit like a play in other ways as well: the story falls neatly

into two acts, each neatly rounded off by a celebratory dinner, and there will be plenty of dramatic conflict between the two of us before we reach the resolution and reconciliation over that final dinner at the end of Act Two.

A two-hander, then, for Actor and Author, with a mystery, a moral—several morals, perhaps—and a variety of stratagems, pratfalls, reversals of fortune, and painful soul-searchings along the way.

David Burke, now that I come to think about it, would be excellent casting to play David Burke. He has all the right qualities.

I don't know who could play my part.

Not me, though, in this particular story. Thank you. Not me.

ACT ONE

MF:

The story began for me at about nine o'clock one morning the previous January, when Michael Blakemore phoned.

I was surprised at the call. Michael is not a great enthusiast for the bleak dawn hours, and over all the thirty years that we have been friends and all the six plays we have worked on together I don't believe he has ever called when the new day was quite so young. I also knew that he was going to be working that morning, rerehearsing the cast of *Copenhagen* in preparation for moving out of the Cottesloe auditorium at the National onto the somewhat smaller stage of the Duchess. But from the sound of his voice he plainly had urgent news.

A very curious letter had arrived in the morning post, he explained, and he had to read it over to me at once. It came from an address in Chiswick, and was signed Celia Rhys-Evans. "Some weeks ago," Michael read out to me, "as an anniversary treat, my husband and I came to see *Copenhagen* under the mistaken assumption that it was a play about the

capital of Denmark, where we had spent a very happy honeymoon many years ago. Also, we had loved Michael Frayn's
wonderful farce *Noises Off.* You can imagine that, in the
event, our visit to the National Theatre proved a disconcerting experience."

I laughed at the poor woman's misunderstanding.

"I know," said Michael. "Very funny. But wait, wait!
There's more to come."

Something in the play had finally caught Mrs. Rhys-
Evans's flagging interest—the long speech in the first act in
which "the German man" talks about his stay at Farm Hall.
"This was clearly the same house which we had lived in for
a short time in the 60s," she said. "We didn't stay long
because it was very cold and damp: no central heating. We
knew nothing about its wartime role, but while we were
there, and in the course of some refurbishings, we did come
across some pages in German under one of the floorboards
in the attic. We kept them at the time, because the children,
who were quite young, were intrigued by them.

"I felt quite sure that they had gone with us when we
moved out of there, but we have only recently been able to
lay hands on them. I have no idea what they are about but
you might as well have them, as otherwise they will only
end up on the compost heap. There were many more pages,
but I'm afraid they have gone the way of all flesh.

"Please let me know if they should prove significant, but
feel free to make what use you will of them."

Enclosed with the letter, said Michael, were two crumpled
and torn sheets of paper, handwritten on both sides in
German. Not knowing any of the language, he had merely
glanced through them—but at once two very familiar names

had leapt out at him: Diebner (one of the German physicists interned at Farm Hall) and Rittner (the British officer in charge of them). There was also an even more familiar phrase: uranium 235, the fissile isotope that the German team had had such difficulties in separating, and at least one formula containing the letter U, the chemical symbol for uranium.

I saw why Michael had phoned at nine o'clock in the morning. I went straight round to his house, collected the text, and began work on it at once.

It was obviously going to take some time. The first few words on the recto of each page were easy enough, because the sheets had evidently been torn out of some kind of British ledger, perhaps a log of incoming and outgoing messages with code words, and had four column headings written in English capitals:

But then the difficulties began. Like Michael, I could pick out some familiar landmarks—Diebner, Rittner, uranium 235. But although I can read printed German fairly fluently, I found the handwriting remarkably opaque. It began reasonably straightforwardly:

But thereafter it became harder. The problems were compounded because the pages were very crumpled and worn by folding, and because in places the writing had been washed away by damp. Even where I could decipher the words I could make no sense at all of some of the syntax. Slowly I transcribed, marking "[?]" wherever I was doubtful:

> *Allgemeine Hinweise: Bitte lesen Sie diese Anleitung vor Montagebeginn sorgfältig durch. Bewahren Sie die Anleitung als Information für Wartungsarbeiten und zur Ersatzbestellung sorgfältig auf. 10^3 (x + 50[or SO]/Z/100> <[?] 10% Ur × 19t) Die Platten der Automatik-Tischtennis-Tische Art-Nr 7121 sind nicht wetterfest. [?] Col. RITTNER Schützen Sie daher die Platten vor Feuchtigkeit, bzw, setzen Sie sie nicht Uranium 235 unmittelbar Warmequellen aus. Eine Wöbung der Plattenhälften kann die Folge sein. Rittner. Bei etwaigem Verzug Diebner. Bei etwaigem Verzug empfiehlt es sich, die Platten einige Tage auf eine ebene Unterlage zu lagen . . .*

And translated:

> General notes: Please carefully read this introduction before beginning the assembly. Keep the introduction carefully as information for servicing and ordering replacements. 10^3 (x + 50[or SO]/Z/100> <[?] 10% Ur × 19t) The surface sections of the automatic table-tennis table type number 7121 are not weatherproof. [?] Col. RITTNER Therefore protect the surfaces from damp, and for that matter do not expose them

to uranium 235 directly from hot sources. This can
result in warping of the surfaces. In the case of any
possible [?] distortion Diebner. In the case of any possible [?] distortion it is recommended that the surfaces
should be laid on a level base for a few days . . .

It seemed to be some kind of scientific joke. One of the
interned physicists had evidently entertained himself, or the
rest of the team, by writing out the instructions for using a
table-tennis table as a parody of a pedantic scientific paper.
I was of course disappointed; the references to uranium 235,
etc., had seemed to promise something more—even the rev-
elation that the German team had some secret understanding
of the atomic bomb that they had managed to conceal from
their captors and history.

I was also a little disappointed, I have to confess, at the
joke itself. One of the more depressing and fanciful mani-
festations of British chauvinism is the fixed belief that the
Germans are not blessed as we are with a sense of humor
(though since so few of us can understand German it's difficult to be sure quite how we have discovered this—and I
also wonder quite how exemplary our own sense of humor
would seem to Germans if they didn't understand English,
and if we had to translate all our jokes into German for
them). The ponderous formulations about the danger of the
table-tennis table warping through contact with hot uranium
235 and all the rest of it seemed to confirm the dreariest
prejudices, though. I wondered if perhaps (and here my own
prejudices began to emerge) it was an example not so much
of German humor as of academic humor, and if academic
humor knew no boundaries.

But *was* it a joke? Why were there so many anomalies? Why was Rittner described as a colonel, when anyone who had spent six months at Farm Hall under his command must have known perfectly well that he was a major? Why was the chemical formula spatchcocked so abruptly into the text? Why, above all, was the syntax so bizarre? "In the case of any possible distortion Diebner. In the case of any possible distortion . . ."

Could there be some other message buried in all that humorousness? Could this table-tennis table just possibly be something more than a table-tennis table? Farther down the page I could see a thumbnail sketch:

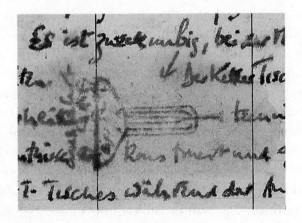

Whatever this represented, it didn't seem to be a table-tennis table, or any part of one.

I struggled on. The table was qualified as being a *Kettler.* I couldn't find this word in my German dictionary. Could it have any connection with the *Ketten* in a *Kettenreaktion,* a chain reaction? Whatever it was, it was plainly something potentially hazardous, since there were repeated assurances that it was "constructed and tested with a view to the most up-to-date safety technology," and that by handling it in the way laid down during the setting-up phase "the risk of injury will be largely excluded." Users were to bear in mind, however, that improper use "may lead to unforeseeable situations and risks, which exclude responsibility on the part of the manufacturer."

The German team is known to have been scrupulous in protecting their laboratory staff from the risk of radioactivity—though they had then gone on to construct an experimental reactor that had no safeguards at all, and that would have killed all the physicists themselves if they had ever managed to get it to go critical. Whatever this *Kettler* was, it seemed to have required instructions framed either in the spirit of the care they had shown for their staff or else in recognition of the dangers they had run themselves.

The next sentence, however, defied any reading I could think of:

"Show anyone you are playing with, particularly Rittner children."

Major Rittner had his *children* with him at Farm Hall? In the middle of an Intelligence operation so secret that no one in Britain was supposed to know of the German physicists' existence? This was the oddest detail in all the oddities so far.

And I hadn't yet struggled to the bottom of the first page.

DB:

I could see that Michael Blakemore was not quite his urbane self as soon as he arrived in the rehearsal room.

He is a remarkable director; his single aim is to serve the play, without ego, without fuss, without attention-seeking. Quite unusual in this age! Mostly he has an un-hurried and often amused manner, very useful in establishing a relaxed atmosphere in rehearsal. That morning, though, he had an urgent and excited air, and without even asking for a cup of coffee he called us all together, actors and stage management.

"I have something quite extraordinary to tell you," he announced.

And he told us all about the mysterious document that had arrived in the post that morning. We were soon all as excited as he was. What seemed most significant to us was that these ancient papers had apparently emerged *from under the floorboards*. As Sara said: "You don't put papers under the floorboards without some good reason. What do you think they say, Michael?"

"I've passed them on to Michael Frayn," said Blakemore. "He can read German. He's trying to decipher them right now. But I could see the name Diebner mentioned. Also Rittner. There are some formulae or calculations. And a diagram. It looks like a crude sketch of some kind of machine. It could solve one of the central mysteries explored in the play: Did Heisenberg know how to make the bomb, and did he deliberately scuttle it? Even if it doesn't tell us that, it could still be extremely significant in historical terms."

It may be a little difficult for an outsider to understand the excitement we shared. We had lived with these characters for the best part of a year, and the Farm Hall episode was a crucial part of their story. Every time we performed the play, I would listen to Matthew's long speech in the first act about their stay at Farm Hall half a century ago—"It's like a pre-war house-party—one of those house-parties in a play, that's cut off from any contact with the outside world . . ."—and I would find myself ruminating on their lives there. I had come to feel a sharp sympathy for them. They had, after all, come through the trauma of struggling to work amid the ruins of a Berlin battered by months of Allied bombing, of failing to build even a reactor, let alone a bomb, and of losing the war. Then they had been rounded up and kept in isolation from the world, not allowed to communicate with their families, or even to know why they were being held. Onstage each night I would find myself trying to imagine some of the detail of their daily routine. We know they played cards and table tennis, and that Heisenberg gave them recitals of Beethoven piano sonatas. I couldn't help wondering if boredom had perhaps tempted any of them into the world of practical joking, either among themselves or at the expense of their British captors—apple-pie beds, water bombs, false alarms—anything to relieve the repetitive routines of a captive existence.

Perhaps these new documents would turn out to cast a little more light on their lives at Farm Hall. By this time Frayn had been working on them for an hour or more. I suggested that Michael Blakemore should ring him and find out what he had discovered. Sara had a mobile phone (there's always someone in a company who has). We all stood around while Michael made the call, trying to guess from the look on his face what Frayn was telling him.

"He says it's very difficult to decipher," Michael reported at last. "It's written in a very strange, dislocated, almost dysfunctional way. But he thinks it's instructions for putting up a table-tennis table."

There was a silence in the rehearsal room.

"A table-tennis table?" repeated someone, sounding almost as disconcerted as Lady Bracknell was by the handbag.

"Very strange," said Blakemore. "But Michael thinks that it could be a code for something."

This was extremely difficult to take in. There was obviously a much more prosaic explanation for it all that no one had mentioned yet.

"Michael," I said, "you don't think it could be simply a hoax?"

Blakemore, though, was able to reject this possibility out of hand. "David," he said, "you haven't seen these papers. I have."

There was no arguing with this. Actors are, after all, quite used to directors who have their own personal vision of a text.

Work came a little hard that day. Curiously enough, I found my mind turning more to the Welsh lady with the double-barreled name. Why had she hung on to the papers all these years if she didn't think they were important? What sort of a person was she?

MF:

I think I've had more letters about *Copenhagen* than about anything else I've ever written. There have been letters from scientists, historians, and philosophers, mostly interested and supportive, occasionally critical, or suggesting improvements to the physics, the mathematics, or the historical record. There have been moving letters from people who knew Heisenberg or the Bohrs, or who had experienced at first hand the agonizing dilemmas of life in a totalitarian state. There have been poems from poets, plays from playwrights, enthusiasms from enthusiasts, madnesses from madmen. But as I worked on it that morning, then asked people for help with it over the next few weeks, and told everyone I met about our mystifying discovery, it became plain that this document from Mrs. Rhys-Evans was by far the oddest communication yet.

It was not only the syntax that was bizarre. There were a lot of simple misspellings: *bedeken* for *bedenken, Mitspeiler* for *Mitspieler, zofort* for *sofort*—with some words (*zilliespiel,* for instance) so malformed as to be incomprehensible. The

pages seemed to have been written by someone who had
been brought up to write German (and who could write
quite naturally the cursive β, the double *s* that English students of German stumble over) but who had either never
managed to become fully literate in the language or was
quite markedly dyslexic. Could any of the physicists have
survived in his profession with this degree of handicap? It
plainly wasn't written by Heisenberg himself, at any rate;
besides being a physicist and a gifted pianist, he was a classical
scholar and a highly literate writer. I imagined some kind of
idiot savant—which might help to explain the clumsiness of
the humor—but on the whole it seemed to me more likely
that the author was not one of the internees. I began to
formulate a theory that he had been one of the British staff—
a German exile, employed because he was a native German
speaker, who had come to England as a child and never
learned to write the German language properly.

I hoped the sense of it all would become clearer as I
struggled on. It became not more but less comprehensible,
though. The tangles of the prose gave way to baffling lists:

> *Sofort: aus zwei Seitenteilen der Aufnahme*
> > *Führung*
> > *Plattenhalften*
> > *Verbindungsrohre*
> > *Ur*
> > *Stabilisiert* ✓
> > *Seitenteile*
> > *Lenkrollen 13 . . .*

Laboriously I looked up the technical terms, but without
a context it was impossible to make much sense of them:

Immediately: from two sidepieces of the take-up
                   guideway
                   surface sections
                   connection tubes
                   [?] *Ur*
                   stabilized ✓
                   sidepieces
                   steering rollers 13
                   locking device ✓
                   tubular braces ✓
                   [?] *Ausschweichen*
                   locking mechanism
                   stirrup 3
                   securing—on
                   steering rollers 32 ✓
                   locking device?✓ or ?P
                   stirrup 9 ✓
                   supporting arms
                   sidepieces of the transport vehicle . . .

The tick next to "stabilized" was reassuring. But the hypothesis that the "table-tennis table" might actually be a table-tennis table seemed to be becoming increasingly unlikely. Could any imaginable table-tennis table involve as many components as this, or such complications in setting it up and using it safely? And what was *Ur*? The German for uranium is *Uran,* and the chemical symbol is U. A lot of words in German begin with the syllable *Ur* to indicate something primeval, original, or simply very old (*Urwald, Ur-Faust, uralte* brandy, etc.), but none of them stops at that point.

Unless, it occurred to me, Ur of the Chaldees had the same name in German. I looked up Genesis in the Lutheran translation:

Da nahm Tharah seinen Sohn Abram und Lot, seines Sohnes Harans Sohn . . . und führte sie aus Ur in Chaldäa, daß er ins Land Kanaan zöge, und sie kamen gen Haran und wohnten daselbst.

So in German, too, Terah took Abram and Lot, and the rest of his family, and they "went forth with them from Ur of the Chaldees, to go into the land of Canaan; and they came unto Haran, and dwelt there." Could some reference be intended to the way in which Heisenberg had taken the rest of the team, together with their prototype reactor, and gone forth with them from Berlin and the British air raids, to go into the land of Swabia; and how they had come unto Hechingen, and dwelt there?

Or for that matter to the way in which Major Rittner had taken Heisenberg and the rest of the German team, and gone forth with them from Rheims of the Champagnes (where they were first held), to go into the land of Huntingdonshire; and how they had come unto Godmanchester, and dwelt there?

I could see that this interpretation was a little far-fetched. But then so was every other interpretation.

On the next page was another list:

Assembly 1 Check
         2 Once   Departure

3 Annually

4 Keep

What? Then a third list:

5	Model	7121-1000
7	"	7122-1000
9	"	7123-1000
11	"	7124-1000

The handwriting became harder and harder to read, the syntax more and more confused, the untranslatable words and my despairing question marks more and more frequent:

> The *Kettler* table is [?] with a view to the most up-to-date safety technology information and the pocket of the table which for [?*den Stichtungfaht desta*β]> can show one two three > in the first place [?*tisiguiniat*] that is [?*ekoj: "rorrein egauqual." Sat it?*]. [*Die des*] must and [?] should become. Guarantee [or: "Take possession."]

By the time I reached the last page I was reduced to:

> [?] Assessment—[?]—[?] [?] [?] [?] [?] [?] >[?] for the game [?] for [?]Tennis-places.
> Can
> step [?*occur*]
> by Rittner—for [?] clasp shoes
> [?]
> Children's TTT 7161-000/7121-000

Possible—[?]—possible
Table T.T. must carefully
[?]

strengthen the surface section retaining stirrups for that
is too [?] under ff.
In the first place a
[?]

Michael Blakemore and I agreed that he would write back
to Mrs. Rhys-Evans to acknowledge receipt of the document while I studied the text in greater detail; I was beginning to feel that making sense of all this might require the
kind of time and effort that was put into cracking the
German Enigma codes at Bletchley Park. I showed the text
to a young German academic and his girlfriend who happened to be in London. They studied it carefully and at
length, and I was gratified to find that they were as baffled
as I was. They found it difficult to believe that any German,
however dyslexic, however early his native education had
been interrupted, could write as confusedly or spell as badly
as this, but agreed reluctantly that the mistakes were not of
the sort made by foreigners struggling to learn German, and
that the fluency of the cursive β was convincing evidence
of real native roots.

They produced one helpful piece of information, though.
There was no mystery about the word *Kettler*—it was the
name of a well-known German firm that manufactured
sporting goods. So perhaps a "table-tennis table" was, after
all, simply a table-tennis table.

But if it was a *German* table-tennis table that was being

so elaborately set up and maintained, and if, as that list of model numbers suggested, the internees had access to not just one but a whole range of German tables, then the mystery merely deepened. The physicists were interned at Farm Hall from June 1945 until the following January. How could anyone in England—even the War Office, even the most buccaneering of Intelligence operations—have obtained table-tennis tables from the still smoking wreckage of the Reich? In any case, why should they have wanted to? Just to help the Germans feel more at home?

Life at Farm Hall, according to the published transcripts, was certainly made as pleasant for the interned physicists as it could be in the circumstances. But now it was beginning to seem as if indulgence was being carried to almost insane lengths. Table tennis with the commanding officer's children, favorite brand-names of sporting goods flown over from home in the midst of postwar austerity . . .

One of the people who had written to me about *Copenhagen* was Professor Dr. Carl Friedrich von Weizsäcker, the distinguished German physicist who had accompanied Heisenberg to Copenhagen on the notorious trip in 1941, and who had been interned with him at Farm Hall. He was now in his nineties, and living near Munich—so far as I knew, the only surviving member of the team. I sent him a copy of the strange document, and an account of its provenance. "I can't imagine that there is anything very serious at the bottom of this mystery," I told him. "But I do find it intriguing, and if you felt interested enough to offer any comments, or any help of any sort, I should be very grateful."

My German friends had mentioned one other, rather more tentative, possibility, which I tried out on Professor

Weizsäcker. From somewhere at the back of their minds they had dredged up a dim memory that there *was* a word *Ur* in German, and that it was an archaism designating a now extinct ancestor of the cow.

The time had come, it seemed to me, to have a little talk with Mrs. Rhys-Evans. I called Directory Inquiry; she was ex-directory.

Nothing very surprising about this, I suppose, but it meant that I should have to write, and that she could, if she chose, write back instead of phoning. A pity. I was beginning to feel that written communication was not always as informative as it might be.

DB:

I was still in bed when Celia phoned.

"The post's just arrived," she said, "and there's a reply from Michael Frayn! David, I think he believes it! Shall I read it to you?"

Celia Rhys-Evans is my wife's cousin. In real life she is a teacher, and not at all given to the chatty inanities of her fictitious counterpart. As she read Frayn's letter aloud, I could scarcely believe my ears.

The papers, said Frayn, were "immensely intriguing." He then cataloged a list of errors and anomalies almost as long as the document itself, and said he couldn't imagine that there was "anything very serious at the bottom of this mystery." Nevertheless he had sent a copy to Professor Dr. Carl Friedrich von Weizsäcker (!), and would be extremely grateful, he declared, if there was anything more that Celia could tell him about exactly where the papers were found. He sounded almost beside himself with excitement. "Were they loose," he demanded, "or in some kind of container? Roughly how many papers were there altogether? Can you remember anything about the other pages? Were they all apparently in the same handwriting? All written on similar pages of the log? Is there any chance that any of them are still somewhere in your possession?"

Hook, line, and sinker. And begging for more.

The idea of a hoax had first come to me during a performance of the play. If anyone is shocked by this, all I can say is that I know of no actor who is so pure onstage that he thinks only what his character thinks. If he did, he would presumably *become* the character: a form of madness. This may of course be what happens to Hamlet—he puts on an antic disposition, and gets stuck in it. Something rather like this seems to have happened once to an actor who was playing the Prince. Daniel Day-Lewis, as was widely reported in the press at the time, suffered a breakdown in the middle of the performance, and the explanation most commonly offered was that he came to believe that the actor playing opposite him as the Ghost of his father was his *own* father, who had been dead many years; whereupon he abruptly left the stage, never to return, and never to play the role again.

This was not a warning that I am ever likely to forget; I was the Ghost.

Acting is mostly a twin-track mental activity. In one track runs the role, requiring thoughts ranging from, say, gentle amusement to towering rage. Then there is the second track, which monitors the performance: executing the right moves, body language, and voice level; taking note of audience reaction and keeping an eye on fellow actors; coping with emergencies such as a missing prop or a faulty lighting cue. These two tracks run parallel, night by night. If one should go wrong, then it is likely that the other will misbehave too.

I had a painful illustration of this just before we finished our run in the West End. After nearly three hundred performances I was tired, and I suppose that the sight of the finishing tape made me relax. At some point I failed to make one of my moves. Sara told me later that a mobile phone had just gone off in the audience. A second or two later I was standing on the stage not knowing where I was or what I had to say. A black hole had opened up around me. Niels Bohr had vanished from Track One, and an alarmed David Burke on Track Two had to take a prompt from the equally alarmed prompter. The move I had failed to make was tied to the thought and the words; when one went, they all three went.

But there is a third and wholly subversive track that intrudes itself at intervals, full of phantom thoughts and feelings that come and go of their own volition. This ghost train of random musings is, of course, to be discouraged, but it can never be entirely denied. As Bohr and his wife, Margrethe, say in the play: "So many things we think about at the same time. Our lives and our physics. . . . All the things that come into our heads out of nowhere." I have been guilty during a performance of dwelling on everything from shopping lists to food fantasies, and I have one particularly alarming idée fixe that afflicts me from time to time. It is the temptation to do or say something so outrageous that it would stop the play, empty the house, and end my career. The specter will appear without warning, like the Ghost itself, and beckon me to follow it over the beetling brow of the cliff: urging me to drop my trousers, or shout obscenities at the leading lady.

So far my guardian angels have succeeded in hauling me back from the brink in the nick of time. But perhaps the thoughts that crept into my head one evening during *Copenhagen* were leading me obliquely in the same direction.

They began innocently enough, during Heisenberg's long speech about Farm Hall. For some reason I found myself thinking this time not about the scientists interned there but about the house itself and the folk who might have lived in it postwar, after the scientists and the British Intelligence officers had long gone and it had returned to a life of humdrum domesticity. I envisioned an ordinary family living there in the sixties without any suspicion of its previous cloak-and-dagger function. Suddenly, without any bidding from me, a couple of plumbers had entered. Before I knew what was happening they were prying up the floorboards, and discovering an old tin box. . . .

Then Matthew came to the end of his speech, it was my turn to speak, and the play rolled on. But I had left my subversive notion parked in a siding, and it was still there the next night—to be shunted a little farther along the track.

Gradually, over a number of performances, my ideas evolved until at last I believed I had a viable plot. Now, who to target? The obvious victim was the author. But I didn't feel I knew him well enough. There is a certain natural distance between an actor and a writer, a mutual shyness. You will meet him at the read-through on the first day of rehearsal, and possibly shake hands, but it is an occasion fraught with nerves and not conducive to the formation of any great intimacy. He will probably reappear when you do your first run-through, by which time you will be so paranoid about his reaction that you will avoid him completely. Michael Frayn himself is the soul of tact, I hasten to add—if only because I now find myself on the other side of the keyboard with him. Nevertheless, a certain hesitation lingers.

It's different with the director. The director one sees on a day-to-day basis, and with Michael Blakemore I had enjoyed a pleasantly teasing relationship as we took turns being rude to each other: the revival of a shared dressing-room partnership in Bristol thirty-six years earlier, when he too had been an actor. Michael has a dry, self-deprecating sense of humor, enjoys a joke, and gives as good as he gets. He, I thought, was my man. I would address Celia's letter to him.

I tried my idea out on my two fellow actors. Sara's generosity onstage and formidable economy I found a nightly acting lesson, but she had just had a most painful bereavement, and she was understandably too preoccupied to give me a moral lesson as well. Matthew made it clear that he disapproved. I felt chastened and put the idea out of my mind. It wasn't until some months later, when I was staying with my sister Rosaleen in Amsterdam, on a short break before we left the National, that I thought of it again. I told my sister about it . . . and she laughed. The power that laughter has over a performer! Once he hears it, all caution is thrown to the winds.

I wrote several drafts of the letter before I was satisfied. I've always believed that a degree of irrelevant detail adds authenticity to a forgery. People don't just tell you the bare facts. Certainly not people like Celia. They like to be expansive. They want you to know something about their lives. They also love a chance to pass judgment. Celia, it turned out, was no exception. I had to force myself, with reluctance, to tone down her worst excesses in the first draft.

I got Rosaleen to copy it in her own handwriting; then, back in England, I addressed myself to the task of creating the German manuscript. It was not such an easy venture. I knew no German, nor anyone who did. And what sort of information was I going to put into it? Something about physics or the physicists, presumably. Then I had a better idea. I would make the thing so absurd that as soon as Frayn translated it, neither he nor anyone else in his right mind could possibly take it seriously. Everyone laughs. Who did this? I did, sir! Naughty boy! And *basta! E finita la commedia!*

I looked for something written in German—anything, the more unlikely the better. One of those instruction manuals for washing machines, perhaps, written in four or five different languages. I searched the kitchen drawers . . . What was this? Instructions for putting up a table-tennis table. A German table-tennis table . . .

I found an ancient ledger that my father-in-law, the late Arthur Calder-Marshall, had used in the thirties and forties for writing his novels. The pages had the right yellowed, brittle look. They had been ruled into columns by some shipping clerk—and the word "code" was even used twice in the column headings.

I filled an old-fashioned fountain pen with some Quink ink and set to work. (What memories of a forties classroom it all brought back!) I chose extracts from the manual at random, broke some of the lines up into vertical columns, added a scattering of familiar names, invented a mathematical formula, and copied a diagram of one of the legs of the table, rotated sideways.

Then I scrunched the paper up in my fist, flicked water on it, and gave it five minutes in the tumble dryer. Now, though, it looked sixty-five years old instead of fifty-five, so I did a little gentle ironing, with the setting on SILK. A deep calm settled on me. Was this what van Meegeren felt when he finished another Vermeer?

And off it all went. Perhaps if Frayn had been the first to see the document, he would have recognized it for what it was. By the time he got his hands on it, however, his hopes had been aroused. Hope is a powerful agent; it's what gets us up in the morning. Then again, where someone else might have seen mere nonsense, Frayn saw ambiguity. Ambiguity is another powerful agent, a great stimulus to the imagination.

And now he wanted more of the same. I shouldn't have provided it. I should have come clean. I knew that's what Matthew Marsh would have had me do. "You're wasting Frayn's valuable time, David!" he would have said. "He's probably writing another play or book—you know what he's like. I think it's all wrong!"

But he *wanted* more!

Perhaps I would have stopped, though . . . But at just this point we moved our wonderful play into the West End, and Trevor Ritchie, who was to be our company manager at the Duchess, introduced us to the new stage management.

"This is Erika," he said.

"Hello," said Erika. Hint of a Northern accent there.
"And this is Petra."
"Hello," said Petra. Another accent—foreign this time.
"Are you Danish, Petra?" I asked.
"German," said Petra.

MF:

Celia Rhys-Evans's reply, when it finally arrived three weeks later, began with a double-edged compliment that seemed as characteristic of what I was beginning to recognize as her style as the chattily offhand put-down in her first letter, and that made me laugh almost as much. She had been in France visiting her son, she said (which was why she hadn't got the letters from Michael Blakemore and me earlier), and had seen a review for the Paris production of *Copenhagen* in the *Figaro*. "It was surprisingly good, but I suppose the French are more intellectual than us, aren't they?"

When I read the next paragraph, however, my amusement gave way to surprise.

"As for the German stuff," she wrote, "it's all very exciting, isn't it: a bit like a John le Carré thriller. And, as you will see from the enclosed, more evidence! When I told my son Micheal (sorry!—another Micheal) . . ."

Another Micheal? I glanced back at the first paragraph. Yes, I had now become Micheal, I saw, and so had

Michael Blakemore. Not all that surprising—it's a name that a lot of people have trouble with. But I was taken aback to discover that her own son was also a Micheal. Mrs. Rhys-Evans seemed to have as many problems with spelling as our anonymous German scribe.

Anyway, when she had informed her Micheal about what she had done, he had replied: "But Mummy, you should have told me! I've got tons of that old German bumph!" He had kept it as a child, he had told her, because he was reading a lot of Biggles at the time and thought it might be "spy stuff."

My interest in her literacy vanished abruptly. I turned to the end of her letter—and there was one of the pages her son had preserved.

It was another leaf torn from the same British signals log, also handwritten in German on both sides of the paper. The writing, however, was completely different from the neat, self-contained, and barely legible script in the earlier pages. It was bold and sprawling—and it was easy to read. I glanced quickly through it. This second author plainly had no difficulties with the German language. There were no mathematical formulae, diagrams, or lists of technical terms, nor any references to uranium or table-tennis tables. This new page appeared to be part of an entry from some kind of journal of daily life at Farm Hall, and it began in the middle of a sentence:

No problems in deciphering *this:*

> . . . *Ende der Woche geklärt sein muβ. Gerlach beschwert sich ohne Ende, wie barbarisch wir hier behandelt werden* . . .

Or in understanding it:

> . . . must be settled at the end of the week. Gerlach complains endlessly about how barbarically we are treated here . . .

No problems, either, in knowing whom this referred to. Walther Gerlach was the Nazi Government's administrator of the German nuclear program, even though he seems to have understood very little about nuclear matters.

> . . . He was sitting on the veranda and consuming a banana (!) while he went on about "these people." "When the war is over we shall take them to the international court. They have no right to hold us here without informing us of the reason. We are not criminals. We are not even soldiers!!" He's downright comic! W said to him: "How many English people do you think are getting bananas to eat at the moment?" He replied: "No idea—nor does it interest me in the least." Typical . . . !

Who was the fair-minded "W"? Presumably either Weizsäcker or Karl Wirtz.

> . . . Recently there was even Champagne. It was O's
> birthday . . .

No ambiguity with this one. There was only one "O" at
Farm Hall, and that was the great chemist Otto Hahn, who
in 1939 in Berlin had done the crucial analysis that detected
the barium in the products of the uranium that Fermi had
bombarded with neutrons in Rome four years earlier, and
so established that its nucleus had fissioned, and transmuted
the heavy uranium into lighter elements.

> . . . There was only a thimbleful each, but after all it
> was kind of Rittner to take the trouble. We raised our
> glasses and sang that silly "Happy Birthday" song. O
> had tears in his eyes. G refused to drink—I emptied
> his glass for him. In the evening we had our usual
> reading, as on every Wednesday. Rittner said: "I'm
> going to read a famous passage from Dickens . . ."

Another familiar point of reference. Major Rittner, according to Otto Hahn in his memoirs, used to read Dickens
to the internees to improve their English, though Hahn remembered the readings as taking place in the afternoon.

> ". . . It's about Little Nell and what happened to her."
> He read aloud for a rather long time. Every now and
> then he paused and pointed out English grammatical
> peculiarities to us, such as, for example, "subordinate
> clause" and "hyperbole." But we were much too much
> taken up with the story, which was really sad, so that
> we were all affected by tears. Rittner reached the end

and said: "We have here a good example of 'pathos' and/or 'bathos,' " (the former means more or less sympathy, the latter slipping into the ridiculous)—it depended upon our point of view. He concluded with "Good night, and enjoy your cocoa." The maid prepared the cocoa for us soon afterward and said: "My goodness, what's the matter here, then? You all look so down in the mouth. Here, drink up your cocoa and you'll soon feel better." These English people—so heartless—have nothing in their heads beyond *bodily* well-being.

By now I felt a little like Heisenberg that famous night on Heligoland when he first realized that the mathematics of quantum mechanics were working out, and had the sensation, as he recalls in his memoirs, of looking through the surface of atomic phenomena at a hidden interior world. Heisenberg found this new world of mathematical relationships inside the atom strangely beautiful. It was the strangely childish banality of the human relationships inside this hidden world of Farm Hall that I felt I was at last glimpsing, and that I found so touching.

I read on, and now a rather more disturbing aspect of this world began to emerge:

The business with the keys is very annoying. I've now been talked to about it by Capt. M for the third time. Always very politely, but there is no doubt that he is concerned. I am under suspicion because I use the gymnasium more often than all the others. This is what is claimed, anyway. But H and W are in there very early in the morning, sometimes even before the guards are up. . . .

I could find no mention in the transcripts of any "Capt. M" at Farm Hall, but the letters "H" and "W" leapt out at me. "H" could have been Hahn or Harteck, just as "W" could have been Wirtz. But together, particularly involved in some kind of private conversation, they were almost certainly Heisenberg and Weizsäcker, who had always been close.

. . . What are they doing there? Whenever I get there they're merely conversing. No exercises—merely intense conversations. On my entrance I always have the feeling that they are changing the subject.

I recalled that it was through his conversations with Weizsäcker that Heisenberg had first become interested in the philosophical implications of quantum physics. Was it philosophy they were talking about so early in the morning in the gym, before the guards were up? Or was it some more delicate subject? It had after all been Weizsäcker who made the sinister discovery that sent Heisenberg on his trip to Copenhagen. He had realized, as Fritz Houtermans had independently, that if they could once get the reactor they were building to go critical it would produce plutonium, and that with plutonium at their disposal as an alternative to the uranium 235 that they still found impossible to separate they would be faced after all with the practical possibility of

manufacturing nuclear weapons. Were Heisenberg and
Weizsäcker now talking secretly about things that they had
not shared with the others, or revealed to their captors?

> . . . The rules lay down that the keys for the gymna-
> sium must be fetched from the house and taken back
> there. Why are they so significant? It could be that the
> keys open other doors as well. Perhaps the guards use
> them even. I have the suspicion that some of the guards
> are making "unofficial" visits to the village. We of
> course are not allowed out, apart from planned "ex-
> peditions to the woods," for gathering mushrooms or
> picking flowers and such. One further thing: during
> these conversations there is always an interpreter pres-
> ent, even though most of us speak English reasonably
> well. But *every time* it's a different interpreter. How
> many "interpreters" have they got here? What do they
> all do? Something is going on here, and I should very
> much like to know what! Do they want to secretly
> murder us one night, or will the crazy English suddenly
> shout "April fool"? The English sense of humor is
> something that I could write whole volumes about—
> but no one would laugh.

And on this melancholy note the extract ended.

There were a number of surprising revelations to take in.
I knew from the transcripts that some of the Germans had
feared at one point that they had been brought to Farm Hall
to be quietly murdered, but I had not realized that there
were guards and interpreters there. According to the tran-

scripts, the physicists had simply been required to give their word not to try to escape, and the eavesdropping team understood German perfectly well without interpreters.

Even more puzzling, though, was the reference to Otto Hahn's birthday. The German team was kept at Farm Hall from July to January, and Hahn's birthday was on March 8. Puzzling as this anomaly was, it was perhaps only to be expected; one of the themes of my play, after all, was the baffling irreconcilability of so much of the historical evidence from the beginning of the story to the end.

Where had his birthday shifted to? There was no indication of the date of the extract. And who had written it? Not Gerlach or Hahn, evidently, nor, if my reasoning was correct, Heisenberg or Weizsäcker. I wondered whether to ask Weizsäcker for his opinion on this new document. I'd had a reply by this time to the letter I'd sent him about the first one. He recalled playing table tennis at Farm Hall, but the fact that they were interned, he reassured me carefully, meant that they had had "no uranium at [their] disposal." Apart from the table tennis, he said, they had scarcely any possibilities for sport apart from running around the garden. There was no mention of any gymnasium. Would the diary extract jog his memory? Would he recall any early-morning meetings there with "H"?

First, though, I decided to fax the new page to Thomas Powers, the author of *Heisenberg's War,* the wonderful book in which I'd first read about the trip to Copenhagen, and which had first set me thinking of the play. I had some dim recollection of his mentioning a diary . . . and, yes, there it was in his footnotes. It had been kept by Karl Wirtz. Wirtz seems never to have published it, but had shown it privately to Powers.

When I got through on the phone to Powers at his home in Vermont, he said he couldn't remember the Wirtz material, and that in any case the style of the extract suggested not Wirtz but another of the team, Erich Bagge, whom Powers had met, and who had seemed to him "slow, correct, and innocent." He had a vague feeling that after the war Bagge and Gerlach had collaborated on a book, and that this book had drawn on a diary kept by Bagge. I dived back into his notes. Yes—*Von der Uranspaltung bis Calder Hall* (Hamburg: Rowohlt, 1957), though it was written not with Gerlach but with Kurt Diebner and Kenneth Jay. And indeed Powers quoted from the diary itself, though without giving any details of publication.

So perhaps all this material was known already. But in that case, why was it hidden under the floorboards? Why hadn't Powers, or anyone else who had written about Farm Hall, mentioned any of the details that emerged from this extract? Had Bagge perhaps lost or abandoned part of his manuscript when he was released? Where could I find the ancient *From Uranium Fission to Calder Hall*? Or even the published version of the diary itself, if there was one?

By this time I had told everyone I knew about Mrs. Rhys-Evans and her strange treasure trove—told them not once, but twice, three times, four times, as I brought them up to date on the latest developments, difficulties, and theories. I was obsessed with the subject. I couldn't wait to get my hands on the rest of the material.

There was a slight problem here, however. The problem was Micheal, Mrs. Rhys-Evans's curiously spelled and plainly rather difficult son. "I'm terribly sorry," she explained in her letter, "but he will only agree to release one page at a time, on condition that you sign a piece of paper, also enclosed, to acknowledge that all the papers belong, as of right, to the Rhys-Evans family, and may not be used without their permission. I'm sorry about this! He's always had a suspicious streak."

And indeed she had enclosed the piece of paper spelling out this agreement. In fact, she had enclosed it in triplicate. It wasn't clear to me that the copyright belonged to anyone in the Rhys-Evans family; it was presumably with the authors, if by any chance they were still alive, and if not then with their heirs. I couldn't see how my acknowledgment of the Rhys-Evanses' possession of a right they couldn't possibly in law possess had very much meaning. But I had become even more eager to see them; it had occurred to me that the story of their finding, and of the new light that it cast upon a minor but intriguing corner of this century's history, might make a rather nice little book.

So I signed. In triplicate.

DB:

I was beginning to find Frayn's replies even more amazing than he found my forgeries.

He had actually signed up to it. In writing. In triplicate. He also thanked Mrs. Rhys-Evans for her "charming letter," and for her "even more astonishing and intriguing news" that there were more of the papers still extant. He would absolutely love to see them, he said. He went into the question of copyright. He promised to make no use of the papers without Mrs. Rhys-Evans's permission. He couldn't imagine that they had any commercial possibilities, he said solemnly, but promised that if it ever did seem possible to write anything about them, then he would of course consult her first, then credit her as the source and come to some arrangement about payment that she felt was fair.

Was there no end to his gullibility? And he was evidently eager for yet more!

I was awestruck by the sheer amount of scholarship that he was employing in following every slightest clue. And the time he must be spending on it! Matthew was quite right: I should be ashamed of myself. But I wasn't! All my earlier scruples had vanished! Was I turning into an Iago or a Richard Crookback? Was this precisely the feeling that explained their fiendish addiction? The joy of power? Is this what a criminal feels when he hears that the full resources of Scotland Yard are being mobilized to track him down? Great! he thinks, I'll send them another couple of clues, and enjoy *Crimewatch UK* tonight, sipping my cocoa as the sniffer dogs go charging off in the wrong direction.

One of the things that was driving me on was having a real-life German on hand to connive with. I felt like a general who has been dithering about his battle plans until suddenly reinforced, out of the blue, by an entire armored division. Petra Abendroth had been brought up in East Germany but had lived in Britain for the last seven years. So she was fluent in both languages. She had been trained as a commercial artist, and among her skills was—calligraphy! She even had a collection of old pens handed down by her grandfather, who had been an expert in that field. Just once in a while you have the feeling that someone up there is actually trying to suggest something to you. After Petra had got over the shock of being asked by a comparative stranger to assist in a forgery, she became a keen and expert co-conspirator, with that attention to detail one has come to expect from anyone German. *Vorsprung durch Technik,* as the Audi advertisements used to say.

She was also very discreet, and kept her secret within the busy corridors of the theatre like a Carmelite nun. One hint of what I was up to, and the game would be up. Matthew Marsh was the only other person within the theatre who was privy to my backroom activity, but I felt confident that, having washed his hands of any role in the conspiracy, he would keep his distasteful knowledge to himself. The Duchess is a small and intimate theatre, though, and my business meetings with Petra must sometimes have had the appearance of a venal British football manager receiving a "bung" from an agent of one of the German clubs. No doubt there was gossip, but I was fairly confident that it would be barking up the wrong tree.

The trouble was that I could not impose on Petra, my hardworking accomplice, to translate more than one sheet at a time, which is why I needed Micheal (by the time I noticed Celia's hazy grasp of her own son's name, the letter had already gone to press), so that he could demand, like the extortionist he was, to be paid one page at a time. As soon as he made his appearance, though, I recognized the birth of a potential star; I realized why writers take black sheep to their bosoms. I had big plans for him. I took care to place him at an unidentified location in France, well beyond Frayn's investigative tentacles—a tax-dodger who couldn't afford to return to Britain. I was beginning to feel the strangely powerful bond that forms between a writer and his characters. Micheal's violent, unpredictable nature, it seemed to me, would be very useful to me as I improvised in response to any efforts Frayn might make to challenge him. If he ever did.

I was being egged on by another accomplice, too: the fictitious version of Celia. She was taking me over! And giving me excellent advice. "Keep it vague!" she told me. "Avoid the specific! More smoke! More smoke!" Frayn's fevered scholarship, she assured me, would take the story into wilder realms of fantasy than any I could imagine. She understood the principle on which fortune-tellers operate: Don't be too specific! Tell a lady that she's going to meet a seven-foot Turk with a Glaswegian accent off the 5:32 from Paddington and she's going to be disappointed. Tell her that she is going to meet a tall, dark stranger and you leave scope for our old friend Ambiguity to work his spell.

On the other hand, advised Celia shrewdly, I should allow the occasional specific detail to emerge through the smoke. So I let the tin box that had housed the papers come suddenly into focus. Celia and her husband recalled that the papers had been "in an old tin box full of rusty bits and pieces. We both remember that among the broken hinges and bent screws there was a very old yellowed table tennis ball. It was fatally dented, as if someone had walloped it in anger. We gave it to the cats to play with and that was the end of that." I could just see Frayn salivating over the possibility that his hero, Heisenberg, had administered the mortal blow. But the picture on the lid of the box, which Celia clearly recalled as being of a couple of old shire horses, her daughter (now living in Australia) remembered equally clearly as being of Shirley Temple. The uncertainty of memory—the way different people's recollections can exist in distinct and different states, rather like quantum particles and Schrödinger's cat—is one of the central themes of the play, so I guessed that this would attract Frayn, too.

I confess, though, that I had become very reckless by this time. The German physicists all spontaneously bursting into tears at the death of Little Nell was dangerously over the top. So was Celia's telling Frayn that he should change the title of his play to something sensible, like *When Scientists Clash!* or *When Boffins Bang!* The explanation I found for why she had now taken to typing her letters was even wilder. (I couldn't keep sending them to my sister in Amsterdam to copy out—though it might have been interesting to see what Frayn would have made of the Amsterdam postmark: "Aha! The Spinoza Gambit!") Celia coolly announced that she had sprained her hand "opening a tin of cat food."

Perhaps it was my death wish, or at any rate my wish to be caught. I was getting a thrill out of living dangerously. In any case it didn't seem to matter—Frayn would believe absolutely anything. I was enjoying myself like a child on a new bike freewheeling downhill. My wife says that a look of dreamy preoccupation would come over me. "I've just got to catch up with some paperwork," I would murmur as I sloped off to my word processor. And she would know that Celia had stolen into the house and taken possession of me once again.

The bills and business letters I should have been dealing with would pile up for days while I communed with my muse. But then I wasn't really writing for Frayn at all by this time. I was writing to entertain myself.

MF:

"I am negotiating with my son for another page to send you. It would be helpful if I could offer him some monetary inducement . . ."

Of course. I should have seen it coming. My expression of interest had gone to their heads. This monstrous pair had suddenly jumped to the conclusion that they were sitting on a gold mine. And they knew that they had the whip hand. I wanted the papers—they had them. They were going to sell them to me one at a time. I couldn't guess how much they would accept for the next page, or how many pages there were to come after that. I was reasonably certain, though, that whatever I paid for this next page I should pay more for the one after, and more still for the one after that, in an arbitrary and indefinite progression until either my curiosity or my resources were exhausted.

Or my years on this earth, since there was no knowing how protracted this drop-by-drop blackmail would turn out to be.

They had me over a barrel.

What neither the disingenuous Celia nor her grasping Micheal could know was that I had another reason of my own to find my helpless frustration galling. I realized that I was in almost exactly the same situation as the central character in the novel I had just finished writing, *Headlong*. The hapless Martin Clay is trying to acquire a picture that he privately believes to be a particularly precious Old Master. It belongs to a so far unsuspecting but entirely venal neighbor, who is hoping to use Martin's discreetly expressed interest for his own shabby ends. Martin slowly discovers the terrible strength conferred by possession, and the terrible weakness implicit in coveting. The price that he will have to pay for the picture, in indignity and moral compromise if not in money, goes up from one day to the next.

There is great pleasure in inventing frustrations and humiliations for one's characters; this pleasure turns rather sour, however, when one finds that one is being subjected to those same frustrations and humiliations oneself. The biter bit has more to endure than the pain of the teethmarks.

I plainly couldn't submit to this extortion. Like Martin, I should have to swallow down my impatience and rage, and feign as much indifference as I could. I composed a discouraging reply, affecting to believe that Mrs. Rhys-Evans's demand for money was really a request for advice as to whether *she* should pay her son money (I said it didn't sound a very practical way to go about it), and offered further advice, unsolicited, as to how *she* should go about realizing the value of the papers. I told her that she would have to establish, at her own expense, the ownership of the copyright and the authenticity of the documents; after the fiasco of the

Hitler diaries, I said, everyone in the business was extremely wary of supposed secret German documents that suddenly came to light.

I told her how few copies even the original Farm Hall transcripts had sold, and I suggested that, even after all her efforts and expense, these new documents on the same subject would be unsalable unless there turned out to be something written in Heisenberg's hand making it clear that he *did* know all the time how to make an atomic bomb. But this, I suggested, was about as likely as a snowstorm in the Sahara, and I asked her what else there could possibly turn out to be that was of interest. "I can't really think of anything," I said sarcastically. "Can you? A secret message from Hitler? The formula for the elixir of life?"

I offered, reluctantly, to look through the papers and advise her, provided she got hold of all of them, and suggested the names of two scientific libraries that might take them off her hands if she preferred. Martin Clay, the increasingly disingenuous hero of my novel, would have recognized the tone, I think.

There was also another pill to swallow. I should even have to be tactful about Mrs. Rhys-Evans's literary efforts. Unbelievably, on top of the demand for money, she had turned to writing fiction, and sent me her first effort for my comments. "I have taken you at your word," she wrote, "when you say, in your programme, that the Farm Hall papers, as published, contain material for several scripts. Having always wanted to be a writer, I have begun a work of fiction based on the experiences of the German scientists at Farm Hall, seen through the eyes of the youngest. I'm calling him Hans.

I hope you won't think me too bold if I send you the opening. I would be most grateful for your comments. Please don't pull any punches: I am here to learn!"

The accompanying typescript was headed *Mystery at Farm Hall*. I glanced through it. The third paragraph seemed to be particularly fine:

> The only sound to be heard was the swish of the wind and the mournful cry of a distant bittern. Suddenly I became aware of another sound. Someone was singing. One of us. It was Gerlach, the crop-haired old Nazi . . .

I stopped grinding my teeth for a moment and burst out laughing. It was true that Gerlach had been the Nazi's administrator of nuclear reasearch, but in his photograph in the transcripts he is a silver-haired intellectual in an elegant suit, with a polka-dot bow tie and a flower in his buttonhole.

> . . . In his harsh, cracked voice he was singing an old marching song beloved of the Führer. . . . But then Heisenburg [*sic*] . . . began to sing too, but to a different tune: the "Ode to Joy" from Beethoven's Ninth. Weizacker [*sic*] joined in . . . until the British driver and his mate began to hammer on the partition, shouting "Shut up, you bloody Krauts. You've been beaten. Lie down and die!"

This, I had to concede, was quite wonderful, even by the standards of most unsolicited manuscripts that turned up in writers' postbags. I thanked her warmly for letting me see

it. It was a bit difficult to have any views on it yet, I said
tactfully, because so far we hadn't really quite got to the
story.

"Maybe," I concluded, "you'll find some material for that
in the papers." And I thanked her for the pages she had sent
so far. I had enjoyed the little mystery, I said.

Martin would have been proud of me.

DB:

"Still," conceded Frayn, having been wonderfully sarcastic about the possibility of there being anything of interest in Celia's papers, "you never know. There may be something. Hope springs eternal."

It does indeed. He was of course referring to the hope of profit he had detected in the grasping Celia and her son. But what I detected was the hope still springing in *him*. He was struggling to keep my hope alive, so that I would send him some more papers. I had to keep *his* hope alive. He was clearly in agony at the possibility of losing the treasure galleon that had only just appeared on the horizon, and that now seemed in imminent danger of being captured by the perfidious Celia and Micheal Rhys-Evans and vanishing back over the horizon flying the skull and crossbones. Behind the polite phrasing and elaborate signals of disinterestedness I could plainly see a man on his knees hoarsely whispering, "Please don't do this to me!"

I was touched. I decided to put my Micheal's demands for money on the back burner. (And what would I have done if Frayn *had* sent me a check? Even *I* might have been embarrassed by that.) I would send the poor man something more, and I would do it for nothing.

Send him *what,* though? I hadn't prepared my next page of German manuscript, let alone given it to Petra. We were both very busy around this time with our own private lives, so I had to think up something else.

By 1945, I knew, Churchill had begun to worry about Stalin's nuclear ambitions. One of the reasons the German physicists were hidden away by the British was to stop them either defecting to the Russians or being kidnapped by them. I decided to investigate the possibility that they had had secret dealings with the Russians.

I didn't know Russian myself, but I knew two people who did, and who between them could probably help me in my researches. One of them was a book-dealer friend of ours, Tony Neville, who had the added distinction of having once conned journalists from the *Express* and the *Mirror* with a story about dubious dealings between the British government and the Russian Department of Trade in defiance of a Western ban on exports of steel to the USSR, which produced panic in the embassies and questions in the British and German parliaments, not to mention a punch in the nose for Tony from the *Mirror* correspondent involved when he found out.

The other person of my acquaintance who knew Russian was Frayn.

Within a couple of days I had discovered (with Tony's help) documentary evidence of Russian involvement! It was very brief and cryptic—only four words on a torn scrap of paper. I felt sure, though, that Frayn would be able to make something of it. He seemed to have an infinite capacity for making something out of absolutely anything I sent him.

The two of us together, with me as a supplier of historic documents and Frayn as the reader of them, were a team that could tackle any problem.

MF:

"In haste," said the next communication from Mrs. Rhys-Evans, a week or so later. "I am so sorry about the enclosed scrap. This is the only sheet of the German bumph my son has sent for you. When I read your last letter to him he said 'This man should be writing WILLS not plays!' He can be very rude. However, I'm sending it on. And you will be glad to know he didn't mention money any more."

I was indeed glad. My policy of firmness and indifference was evidently paying off. The results in practical terms, though, I discovered when I turned to the new "sheet of the German bumph" that she had attached, were somewhat meager. It was the briefest and oddest document yet—a torn-off corner of yellowing newspaper with four words penciled on it in capitals:

Cyrillic characters. **Поставьте пакет вниз береза.** I gazed at the words in bafflement. I couldn't share Mrs. Rhys-Evans's uncritical acceptance of this as another piece of German—but what language *was* it? I assumed, by analogy with Russian, that it meant "Put the package under the birch tree." It didn't seem to *be* Russian, though. A Russian would be more likely to write **Положите пакет**—"lay the packet"—rather than **Поставьте**—"stand it"—since in Russian you have to choose whether something that's put somewhere is put there upright or on its back. It was possible, of course, that the package in question was one that had to be stood upright. But no Russian could conceivably write **вниз** ("downward") to mean **под** ("under"). The only other languages written in the Cyrillic alphabet are Bulgarian, Serbian, Ukrainian, and Belorussian. I'm not familiar with any of them, but I found it difficult to persuade myself that in any imaginable Slavonic language a plainly oblique case of **береза** would be written in what was equally plainly the nominative form.

So perhaps it *was* Russian—broken Russian written by someone with an even worse command of the language than the author of the first document had of German. Maybe the British authorities at Farm Hall had been employing not only displaced Germans but East European exiles who knew no English or German, perhaps as domestic staff, and with whom either the British personnel or the German inmates had to communicate in a kind of Russian pidgin. . . . But then why had this trivial note to a janitor or cleaner been hidden under the floorboards with the journal and the rest of the material?

I turned the scrap of paper over. It had evidently been

torn out of a publication called *Peace and Freedom News,* with an address in Berkeley, California. My picture of life at Farm Hall changed yet again. There were not only children around, not only an array of specially imported German sporting equipment, but American pacifist publications circulating. No one could have accused the British of imposing a repressive regime upon their distinguished guests.

But *was* American pacifist literature either published or imported so soon after the war? There was no date in the fragment of text remaining. Then I looked more closely at the address . . . and found a zip code.

Whether this little scrap of anachronistic scribble did after all justify my policy of offhandedness now seemed open to a certain amount of doubt. I decided to continue with it, nevertheless, and my reply to Mrs. Rhys-Evans this time was very short and cool indeed. I merely informed her that the words on the front were not German but very bad Russian, then mentioned the existence of the zip code on the back, and noted that zip codes were introduced by the U.S. Post Office Department in 1963.

Which, as I concluded tersely, was a little discouraging.

DB:

The transfer to the Duchess was a success, and within a few weeks Michael Codron and his fellow backers had recouped their investment. Trevor Ritchie, our company manager, popped his head round my dressing-room door.

"Michael Codron wants to take us all out to dinner to celebrate," he said.

"That's nice. When?"

"April first. Okay?"

April first . . . ? At once alarm bells rang. A dinner party where Frayn and I would come face-to-face, on April Fools' Day? He had obviously found out; the game was up. The biter was going to be bit.

I went round to Matthew's dressing room.

"He knows!" I told him. "He's worked it out!"

"It was obviously going to happen sooner or later," said Matthew. "What do you think he's going to do?"

"Make some kind of speech about it, probably. Or trick me back somehow. Leave me with the bill for dinner, perhaps."

"Oh, good. In that case I'll let myself go on the wine list."

I had mixed feelings. Perhaps it was just as well that the game was over. I hoped that my activities had proved entertaining to both of us—though obviously for quite different reasons—and I wouldn't have wanted it to turn sour.

But then again I was sad. I had been enjoying myself—particularly in the strange new relationship with Frayn. It was a fictitious one, and totally different from that of actor-writer, but it had something of the odd compelling quirkiness of the relationships that can arise between detective and suspect, say, or kidnapper and kidnapped. I felt a wonderful freedom, to offer advice, to patronize, to poke fun. Personalities are different on paper. It's like putting on a mask. You can use a different tone of voice from your own, but one that may actually be more comfortable, perhaps even more truthful, than your usual voice—more attractive, more vulnerable, or more powerful. It's like a woman trying out different lipsticks, and making faces in the mirror as she does so: Now I'm demure, now I'm a tramp! Bernard Shaw and Ellen Terry (writer and actress) had such a relationship. They communicated entirely by letter, and it gave them a freedom and a frankness that a face-to-face relationship might have destroyed. They kept the correpondence up for twenty years, and each grew quite fearful of meeting the other.

Now my correspondence with Frayn was over. The face-to-face confrontation was at hand.

On the morning of April Fools' Day my fears were confirmed. A frigid little note from Frayn (as much as to say, "You think you can be brief. Well, try this!") informed me that the scrap of newspaper I had used had been published only after 1963, and that the Russian was all wrong. So this is what had finally finished me—opening the Russian front. I had made the same mistake as Hitler, and Napoleon before him.

The zip code was my mistake. *Peace and Freedom News* had come from Arthur Calder-Marshall's effects once again, but I'm just not very good on dates. The Russian was Tony Neville's fault. Or was it? I had assumed that he was as fluent in Russian as Frayn—he had a Russian mother, after all. Now I found out that though he understands it well enough, he speaks and writes it only imperfectly.

So hubris had been followed by nemesis once again, and we had reached the dénouement of the story, the great public unmasking that comes at the end of so many comedies. The scene was to be set in a restaurant just round the corner from the theatre, housed in a building that Michael Codron said had once been a notorious brothel. It seemed a rather appropriate setting for the stripping away of illusion and false identities.

MF:

I recounted the latest twist in the story to everyone at Michael Codron's grand recoupment dinner on April first. Either they asked me, or else they didn't and I told them anyway. I'd already told almost everyone I knew in London; I couldn't see any reason for not sharing the pleasure with the people most closely associated with the story. One after another I amazed them with the news about the little snatch of impossible Russian on the little scrap of anachronistic American newpaper. I told Michael Codron himself, I told Michael Blakemore. I told the stage management and the front-of-house people. I didn't get a chance to tell Petra, our new German ASM, who would probably have been particularly interested, nor for some reason did I manage to find myself face-to-face with David Burke. But I think I told Sara Kestelman, and I certainly told Matthew Marsh.

I had by now developed a tentative theory to explain the apparent anomalies. According to the introduction to the transcripts, before Farm Hall had housed the German physicists it had served as a safe house for Intelligence purposes.

I surmised that it had reverted to Intelligence after the Germans had been released, and that the scrap of newspaper represented the coincidental overlap of an operation in the sixties to maintain surveillance on the peace movement and another to train agents for surveillance on Russia—much as I had been trained myself during my National Service a decade earlier. I envisaged some of the language trainees writing notes for one another in (perhaps humorously) bad Russian, and doing it on scraps of paper left lying around by their colleagues in the other department.

The question remained, of course, as to how any materials arising like this had come to be found with documents concealed under the floorboards in 1945. But the irreconcilable ambiguities of the historical record were something I had got very used to while I was researching the play. As Bohr says in my text of the apparently inexplicable anomalies that confronted him and Heisenberg when they were studying the structure of the atom in the twenties, they offered a fascinating paradox. Bohr was a great believer in the suggestiveness of paradox.

The only one of my hearers who seemed less than fascinated by all this was Matthew Marsh, when I found myself sitting next to him after Michael Codron made us change places for the pudding. I had expected the problems to have a particular appeal to him. He had embodied the ambiguity and deviousness of Heisenberg as totally as David Burke had the innocence and openness of Bohr, and during rehearsals, to my embarrassment, had spotted a number of errors and inconsistencies in the text. But he didn't seem to be much interested in the ambiguities of the German documents, or the errors and inconsistencies they contained. He watched me with what seemed like growing sadness, and eventually he gave up listening altogether and went off to talk to David Burke.

I was evidently becoming a bore on the subject. That didn't stop me, though. I turned to David Baron, who was David Burke's understudy at the time, and told *him* all about it instead.

D B:

I kept out of Frayn's way all through the great April Fools' dinner, and still the blow had not fallen. Still he had not risen to his feet and pointed the accusing finger at me. I was beginning to relax a little when I became aware that Matthew, who had been sitting next to him, was at my elbow, murmuring something. At once I was on my guard again; he had come to warn me that Frayn was about to begin the great unmasking.

"David," said Matthew. "I've had Michael Frayn going on and on at me about this Rhys-Evans woman and table-tennis tables and keys and birthdays and zip codes and Gerlach and Heisenberg until I think I'm going mad—and I think *he* may have gone mad already! He's totally obsessed by it all!"

I could scarcely believe my ears.

"You mean . . . he *doesn't* know? He *hasn't* tumbled it?"

"No, but, David, this can't go on! You can't let him get madder and madder! Look, it's April first—you can make a joke of it. Just say something to him to put him out of his misery!"

But I'd stopped listening. My brave Frayn was still a believer, a true zealot. Don Quixote was still on his horse, his trusty lance rampant, ready to chase windmills—*my* windmills!—all over the beautiful landscape!

It was as much as I could do to stop myself from brushing Matthew aside and rushing up to Frayn to hug him. And thank him, with tears in my eyes. The show could go on!

What a waste it would have been if it had had to stop! I had assembled a star cast, who were fully rehearsed, nay, were already performing to packed houses! And these were only the previews! Celia and Micheal had as yet shown only a fraction of what they could do; I had all sorts of plans for them. Celia was going to reveal a past rich in all manner of famous boyfriends. As for Micheal, there were no depths to which I would not send him. I had a headlong fall planned for him unmatched since Milton took Lucifer by the scruff of his wings and hurled him down to Hades!

And I'm just talking about what was going to be happening in Celia's covering letters. In the parched and yellow pages of the anonymous chronicler's manuscript, meanwhile, my German cast were rehearsing for a long season at the Whitehall—the old Whitehall that Frayn and I both fondly remembered—with Walther Gerlach playing the Brian Rix part. Then there was my novel (sorry—*Celia's* novel!), based on the excellent literary model of Enid Blyton's *Famous Five,* with dear little Hans braving all sorts of perils to win through in the end and prove himself a second Einstein by discovering an antidote to war! And now it could all go ahead! Their brave, silly, tragic, funny stories could all be told!

"Put him out of his misery?" I replied to Matthew. "What

misery? He's having the time of his life! And so am I! This show could run and run!"

Matthew went away, looking more worried than ever. What had become of my scruples? Was I not being cruel in prolonging the thing in this way? Did I really care twopence if Frayn was wasting his precious time barking (an apt word) up the wrong silly tree? Clearly I did not care twopence.

It dawned on me that I had become addicted—like an alcoholic who has to have one more drink. Except that I knew it was not going to be one more. I had chasers lined up to the end of the bar. I had become a jokaholic! Someday I would have to pull myself together and seek out the local chapter of Jokers Anonymous. But not tonight! The show must go on!

And I can truthfully say that I felt more fond of Frayn than ever. We were in this thing together, after all. We were Morecambe and Wise, Rodgers and Hammerstein. We were the Marks & Spencer of false documents.

MF:

Matthew came back to the table and sat down again. He looked preoccupied, but I at once resumed explaining my theory of the bad Russian.

He at last had a contribution of his own to make to the proceedings, though.

"It was David Burke," he said.

I can't remember now whether I took time to grasp the shattering implications of those four words—whether I had to ask for them to be repeated, and put supplementary questions to Matthew—or whether their meaning burst on me at once, as if it had been hidden inside my head all the time, waiting only to be released.

One way or another, though, everything at last fell into place.

Matthew just hadn't known what to do about it, he said unhappily. He had been deeply uneasy about letting the joke go on, and watching me get ever more entangled, but he felt like a Quisling toward David for telling me.

I don't recall what I said. Nothing very profound, I'm

afraid. I could have remarked upon the fascinating interplay of history and fiction, of deception and credulity, but I didn't. I think I managed a few rueful exclamations. A few rueful smiles, laughs, and shakes of the head. Perhaps a word of thanks. I hope a word of thanks.

I do recall, though, that one even more unsettling thought flashed into my head. I suddenly remembered that it was April first. It couldn't be *Matthew* who had hoaxed me, could it? Or who was hoaxing me even now, by telling me that I had been hoaxed . . . ? Once the ground has shaken beneath your feet, you feel it go on shaking for a long time afterward.

After the pudding, Michael Codron made us change places yet again, and I found myself opposite David Burke. I couldn't think what to say to him. I couldn't even look at him.

He was as friendly as ever.

"So what's happening about all those papers under the floorboards?" he asked me, plainly as fascinated as everyone except Matthew had been. "I gather something's turned up in *Russian* now!"

I agreed briefly that this was so, but didn't expand on the matter. I found myself quite unable to meet his innocently smiling gaze, as if *I* were the guilty one.

"What do you think the explanation is?" he persisted.

I didn't put my theory to him. I didn't say anything. I just did my best to smile back and then changed the subject. I felt bad about my surly unresponsiveness. He sounded so interested, so genuinely eager to know.

ACT TWO

MF:

The hot burn of shame.

That's what my character Martin Clay feels in the novel when he suddenly jumps to the conclusion that the painting he is trying to buy is a forgery, and that he is the victim of a complex confidence trick. I'd got the reaction absolutely right, I noted with a certain professional satisfaction. The hot burn of shame was exactly what I was feeling now—the almost physical sensation of a blush spreading over the whole surface of my body.

I thought of all the people across London I'd told the story to. I remembered all the narrative flourishes I'd employed: the way I'd humorously introduced it with Mrs. Rhys-Evans's disappointment at finding that the play was not a farce about the city where she had so implausibly spent her honeymoon, and then the way I'd dramatically stilled the laughter with my evocation of the mysteriousness of the document she enclosed.

I recalled my earnest, careful letters to Weizsäcker and Powers.

I thought of my delight at the depths of Mrs. Rhys-Evans's naïveté and ignorance—at her belief that the Russian was German, at her description of Gerlach as a crop-haired Nazi, at her inability to spell the name of her own son.

I revisited some of the choicer details. The imported German table-tennis tables. Major Rittner's children. The death of Little Nell.

I reexamined some of my more ingenious explanations of the anomalies. The exiles who were forgetting their native languages. Ur of the Chaldees. The extinct ancestor of the cow.

I remembered David's actually warning Michael Blakemore that it was a hoax—and then his repeating the warning in the journal, with the reference to April Fools' and the English sense of humor.

I recollected my plans to write a book about it all.

I had been made a fool of. Worse—I had eagerly collaborated in the process. I had made a fool of myself.

How long would I have gone on if Matthew hadn't rescued me? What further idiocies would I have swallowed? What further idiocies of my own would I have dreamed up to explain them?

In the days that followed, I recalled something else Matthew had told me. David had assured him, he said, that in the first document he had inserted a clue of childish simplicity that would immediately give the game away if I hadn't seen through it already. I searched through the text again. It took me a long time to find it, even now—and then suddenly it leapt out at me. It was in one of the passages that I had found most opaque, on the last page but one:

. . . sofort tisiguiniat das ist ekoj: "rorrein egauqual." Sat it?

I had misread the cramped and faded handwriting, I realized. With the high-diopter lenses of hindsight I now saw that the relevant words read:

. . . tisigniniar . . . ekoj . . . "rorrim egaugnal." Get it?

I did at last get it. *"Rorrim egaugnal"*—we were going backward, as Heisenberg complains in the play about Schrödinger's attempt to explain quantum phenomena in terms of classical wave mechanics.

"Joke." Yes. Though why it was raining I still didn't understand.

Another thing I could now see with great clarity was the peculiar justice of my punishment. I had spent my life inventing plots and characters, and expecting others to suspend their disbelief. Now here was somebody else inventing them for a change—and an actor, at that, who was supposed to be performing one of *my* characters in one of *my* plots. And what was *I* doing? I was suspending *my* disbelief! No, not just *suspending* my disbelief—hanging it by the neck and jumping on its corpse. The biter had indeed been bit.

How could I have fallen for such a preposterous farrago? Precisely, it seemed to me as I went over everything that had happened, *because* of its sheer preposterousness. I thought—I *hoped*—that I might have been a little more cautious if the instructions had openly purported to be for building an atomic bomb, or if the journal had recorded sinister tears at the death of Hitler. But the instructions for putting up a *table-tennis table*? The record of grown men being reduced to tears by the death of *Little Nell*? No hoaxer could possibly have been idiot enough to try persuading anyone of such nonsense! It could only have been genuine!

Perhaps all successful hoaxes and confidence tricks evoke belief partly by appearing to defy it. The heights of implausibility that have to be scaled serve only to deepen the mystery concealed behind them. In any case, the sheer sense of there being a mystery, of something being hidden beneath the surface, waiting to be revealed, is immensely alluring. I had enjoyed the mystery very much. Everyone to whom I had told the story had enjoyed it.

I certainly recognized, even more ruefully, that the scheme had had the two other classic elements of such tricks. It had appealed to my vanity, and it had aroused my hopes of reward. My vanity was of being able to read the German. I am not a natural linguist, and I was secretly rather proud of having slowly improved my German over the years. And the reward that seemed to dangle before me was the professional satisfaction I should get from the modest but intriguing book that I might perhaps be able to make out of it.

Another pang: it was not the first time that my credulity had been exposed. An earlier occasion came to mind, for instance, that also turned on my knowing a little German. My wife and I had once been approached in the streets of Istanbul by a criminal-looking man with sinister blue lips. I had accepted his entirely unnecessary offer to guide us to the Blue Mosque, in spite of my wife's very plainly expressed misgivings, because he spoke a few words of German, which he had learned as a *Gastarbeiter* at the BMW works in Munich, and I was so delighted at being able to communicate with someone in Turkey at last. When we reached the surprisingly desolate and empty piece of waste ground in front of the mosque, he rubbed his finger and thumb together and said: *"Geld."* Thinking he wanted a small tip for his trouble, I got out my wallet and extracted a low-denomination banknote. He made it clear with gestures that nothing was further from his mind than any monetary gain. All he wanted to do was to show me the picture on the banknote.

"Atatürk," he explained

"Atatürk," I readily agreed, since even I by this time could recognize the founder of the modern Turkish state.

"Mehr Geld," demanded our new friend. I handed him another banknote.

"What are you doing?" said my wife in alarm.

It was obvious what I was doing. I was being shown that there was a picture of Atatürk on this one as well.

"Mehr Geld," said my fellow Germanist. I got out another banknote.

"Michael!" cried my wife.

"Atatürk," said the man.

Eventually he was holding all my Turkish banknotes, and had established to my entire satisfaction that there was a picture of Atatürk on every single one of them, from the lowest denomination to the highest.

"Now get them back," ordered my wife urgently, but then of course her lack of German prevented her from sharing the bond of mutual trust that my Turkish friend and I had established.

In any case he had more information about the world's currency to impart to me. *"Englisches Geld,"* he demanded. I handed him a five-pound note. He pointed at the portrait of the Queen. *"Nicht Atatürk,"* he said. He was right again, as I was happy to confirm. *"Nicht Atatürk,"* I agreed, with effortless fluency. *"Mehr englisches Geld,"* he replied. . . .

When finally he was holding all my Turkish and all my British currency, he pointed to a tiny figure in the distance. *"Mein Freund,"* he explained. He indicated by gestures that he was going to take all the banknotes over to this friend and demonstrate to him as well the ubiquity of Atatürk on the Turkish notes and his total absence from the British ones. This seemed to me a small but helpful move toward increasing international understanding, but here my wife dissented with such vehemence that for the sake of marital harmony I was regretfully obliged to decline.

The hot burn, yes. I had felt a touch of it then, after I had reviewed the incident at leisure with my wife and come to see the force of her reservations. I felt it now in full strength—the same great blush spreading not only over my body but down into my very bones.

Then again, life was mockingly imitating not only the events in my novel but the ones in the play as well. Matthew Marsh, it occurred to me, had been put in rather the same position as his character. Like Heisenberg, he had found himself torn between keeping a secret and revealing it— between the demands of loyalty and those of common humanity. Like Heisenberg (if we are to believe his own account of his actions), he had preferred the latter. Like Heisenberg again, he understandably didn't wish to advertise his choice.

It also raised the same questions of motivation. Why had David done it, I wondered, just as Bohr and Heisenberg in the play wonder why Bohr should once have risked his life on a game of throwing stones at a washed-up mine, and why Heisenberg had risked his by balancing on one foot on top of a Japanese pagoda. It even raised the same questions of explaining a failure to do something. Why, asks the play, did Heisenberg fail to do the crucial and obvious equation for the diffusion of neutrons in uranium 235? Why, I now asked myself, did I fail to raise any of the crucial and obvious questions about the documents I had been sent? Heisenberg suggests that his failure was explained by his unconscious reluctance to know the answer, in case it opened the way, as it would have done, to building an atomic bomb. What unwelcome knowledge was *I* trying to keep from myself?

In the taxi on the way back from the restaurant, I broke the news to Michael Blakemore. At least I was able to share my astonishment with him, and also some of my discomfiture—though since he'd relied on me for the translation of the German I felt a certain responsibility for bringing him down with me. We phoned each other a lot in the days that followed to marvel and laugh yet again at the skill and insulting cheek with which David had caught us. And each time, after we'd marveled and laughed, we couldn't help falling silent yet again as we remembered the details of what we'd believed, and the lengths our belief had carried us to.

For both of us the ground had shaken—and went on shaking. I got a phone call from someone I didn't know but who claimed, implausibly, as it seemed to me, to be the son of a friend; it's David Burke, I thought at once. Michael received an unwelcome letter from Inland Revenue, and for a moment dismissed it furiously as another of David Burke's forgeries.

There are a range of questions that have worried philosophers down the ages about how we know that other people have minds and feelings, and how we can be sure that we are living in a real world, and not in a dream, or in a shadowland of mere appearances. Turing's proof of the possibility of a universal computer may bring these ancient worries to life again, because the universal computer is now interpreted by some physicists as being tantamount to a universal virtual-reality generator, which could in theory surround us with a virtual world indistinguishable from a real one. I began for the first time to feel the force of these venerable metaphysical anxieties. Maybe, it seemed to me at times, we are living in a universal virtual-reality generator already, and its name is David Burke.

At this point, possibly, even you—yes, you reading this, who are far too shrewd to be taken in by stunts like the one I fell for, who have never been hoaxed in all your life—perhaps even you begin to feel a faint shadow of unease. Up to now you have assumed that I, at any rate, was telling the truth, and that this was a factual account. You have felt as superior to my ridiculous naïveté as I did to Mrs. Rhys-Evans's. What you're thinking now is that I have been at some pains to remind you of the kind of writing I usually do, which is fiction. Have I said this in the spirit of David Burke's reminding Michael Blakemore in the rehearsal room of the possibility that the documents might be a hoax? Is *this* all a fiction as well?

And this "David Burke" who has apparently been making such a fool of me, and who is now allegedly writing the account of it with me—is even *he* an artfully suggested fiction, my own private version of the real David Burke, just as my Niels Bohr is of the real Niels Bohr?

Be honest with yourself. You did actually believe it, didn't you, when I told you that *I'd* believed all that nonsense about table-tennis tables and Little Nell. You did! You believed that a grown man who writes plays about quantum mechanics was taken in by such childishness! That is the most ludicrous implausibility so far! And yet you managed to believe it! The joke was on *you* all the time!

No, of course not. I was telling the truth before. It's all fact. Up to the last paragraph. And now it's fact again. It is! I assure you! Honestly! Believe me!

Your moment of unworthy doubt is over. I hope. But perhaps you can feel the ground still shifting very slightly under your feet.

DB:

Why did I do it?

Was it some kind of actor's revenge on Them (directors and writers) for various unspecified grievances over the years? Was it an exercise in metaphysics? (What is Reality? What is Truth?)

I'm afraid not. The real reason is simpler, and perhaps duller. I did it for a laugh. It was a joke.

I think it is partly the retarded child in me. I have always been late in doing everything: passing exams, understanding jokes (yes!), losing my virginity, getting married, having a child. So it seems consistent that I should be indulging in the kind of prank that anyone else might have got out of his system before his fifteenth birthday.

Then again, I suspect that I have been trying to make up for a rather solemn childhood—always looking at the ground, or with my head in a schoolbook. I was a grind. I believe I still project a grave presence. It comes in useful in the acting. But it means I don't get offered the comedy that I adore.

My duplicitous correspondence with Frayn, I have to confess, was not my first transgression—or my second, either. This kind of thing has happened before. I must ask for a number of previous offenses to be taken into consideration.

My career as a forger began many years ago, when I was playing a small role in John Osborne's *The Hotel in Amsterdam* with Paul Scofield. Going home on the train to Haywards Heath one night after the performance, Scofield told us, he had met Jimmy Edwards and Sir Laurence Olivier and fallen so deep into conversation with them that the train was drawing out of the station at Haywards Heath before he realized he had arrived; whereupon he had pulled the emergency cord and walked off into the night before anybody could stop him.

The next day, Scofield received a letter from a Sgt. Blenkinsop of the Railway Police. He was wanted for questioning, said Sgt. Blenkinsop, in connection with an incident at Haywards Heath station. Two witnesses aboard the train had insisted on giving their names as "Jimmy Edwards" and "Sir Laurence Olivier," as a result of which they had been taken into custody and held overnight at Brighton police station.

Scofield saw through this immediately, and just as quickly identified me as the culprit. But it gave me some sort of thrill, a small rush of adrenaline, and that was what started me off. Not that I have ever become a serial prankster; the habit has always been under control. Years would sometimes go by between one episode and the next. When the urge came upon me, it would usually take me by surprise.

It struck once when my wife and I were rehearsing and previewing Gorki's *Philistines* for the RSC at the Barbican. Clive Russell, a huge Scots actor, built like Ben Nevis, who was in the production with us, went out and bought himself a wide-brimmed velour hat with which he was so pleased that he kept it on all the time, even during lunch. Then one day he came in hatless and unhappy. At the Shaw Theatre the previous evening, he said, he had for once taken the great hat off while he bought a drink. When he came back, it had vanished. We all did our best to cheer him up, but I decided to offer a little practical help as well, because I remembered the name of the shop where he had bought it.

Two days later, Clive walked into rehearsal with a box under his arm and a letter in his hand, scarcely able to contain himself for excitement.

"Listen to this," he said.

Dear Mr. Russell,
I am returning the splendid hat I stole from you at the Shaw Theatre the other night.

I wanted to add this wonderful specimen to the collection of hats, all 234 of them stolen, which I keep in a special room in my ranch in Texas. I have stolen hats from all over the world: an orthodox archbishop's hat from Cyprus, a French gendarme's hat taken at great personal risk during the student revolt of 1968, a German general's hat taken while he was toying with his mistress. And so on. Yours was only the latest conquest.

But an extraordinary thing has happened. The night after I stole your hat, I visited the Barbican—wearing your hat, of course. Imagine my astonishment when the very man I have stolen the hat from strides on to the stage: you! You speak and reveal that your fictitious father is a singer. So was my real father. That he was a drunkard. So was mine! And finally that his name was Igor Petrovich. My father's name precisely.

The tears are streaming down my face. I realise that my father is sending me a message—from wherever he is. I must return your hat! I must reform my ways! I have been a sinner!

So here is your beautiful hat, with my profound apologies. Enjoy it, and spare a thought sometimes for

The Lover of Hats

Clive looked at us all. I could see that he was deeply moved.

"Clive," I said, "you do realize that it's April first today?"

But nothing could shake his conviction or lessen his emotion. In the days and weeks that followed, he never tired of telling the story and showing the letter to anyone who would listen. My wife often urged me to tell him the truth, but I replied that I shouldn't dream of spoiling the pleasure it all gave him.

A year later, in fact, when we were due to finish the run, the Lover of Hats wrote Clive another letter, with some nonsense or other about flying in from Texas in his private jet to catch Clive's last performance. Clive read it aloud to everyone in the large makeup room at the Barbican—and would believe the story to this day if he hadn't glanced up to savor our appreciation and caught the reflection of my wife in one of the mirrors, stuffing a handkerchief into her mouth, her shoulders heaving. The same old problem—accomplices!

An early prototype for Celia Rhys-Evans called Doreen

Brown came into existence when we were rehearsing Richard Nelson's *New England* in the Pit, the small studio theatre at the Barbican. Angela Thorne had to sit in a rocking chair at the edge of the stage, almost in the laps of the front row of the audience, idly turning the pages of a family photo album. The stage management had found a real album in a junk shop, full of photographs of a real family at different moments of their lives: weddings and birthdays and parties on the beach, in short pants and long pants, nappies and long dresses. As I looked at it during breaks in rehearsal, I began to wonder about this family, just as I did later about the people who must have lived at Farm Hall. I found myself rather touched by the pictures. Other people's families seem to affect me this way.

After the play had opened, Angela Thorne received a surprising letter. She read it aloud to all of us in the green room:

Dear Miss Thorne,

I came to see your play the other night with my sister Mabel. We had been expecting to see *Cats,* but the agency got it wrong. Anyway, your play was much cheaper, so we didn't mind, though we'd have liked a few songs. We had good seats, in the front row, very close to your rocking chair. Mabel suddenly whispered to me—"That's our family album!" And it was! Turned up again after all these years! We were so close we could see it ever so clearly. There was our youngest sister, Tina, in the tutu she wore on her twelfth birthday. She wouldn't take it off, even in bed! Our John was there, dirt all over his face as ever. And Grannie Harbottle—she was a card—loved her Ovaltine. And

Horace. He's the one with the wooden leg. He was our uncle but he came to a bad end. I'm quite surprised he's in the album—I said to Mabel. They were all there—all of us. Except Ethel of course. Mabel and I had a little cry over it in the interval. . . .

We've booked eleven seats in the front row for your Saturday matinee. All the family. Grannie Edgerton is coming up from Margate. They've let her out of the home specially. She thinks we're all going to be stars. So would you mind terribly turning the pages really slowly that day—so we can all have a look?

Yrs, Doreen Brown

The whole company was as moved as Doreen and Mabel had been. The only dissenting voice was mine, once again.

"It's a hoax," I told them confidently. No one paid any attention to my skepticism. If it hadn't been for Angela's nervousness at the approaching matinee and the proximity of eleven members of the Brown family trying to see over her shoulder from Row A, I might not have relented, and told them who the hoaxer was.

It takes two to tango. Without the eager belief of the hoaxee, the hoaxer could achieve nothing.

MF:

The problems that had been preoccupying me for the past couple of months, of how to make sense of the documents and how to extract the rest of them from Mrs. Rhys-Evans and the appalling Micheal, had now vanished like burst bubbles, in the way that apparently intractable problems sometimes do. But now another, and perhaps even trickier, problem took their place: how on earth to extract myself from the situation I had got myself into.

This was the difficulty: I couldn't see how to tell David that he had been blown without also telling him who had blown him, which would plainly be a betrayal of Matthew's confidence. I couldn't leave him to think it might have been Petra, and it couldn't have been Sara because she said she had no recollection of David's ever mentioning it to her. I didn't have the cheek to pretend I'd seen through the deception myself—and even if I had, how would I have explained my guessing that the perpetrator was David Burke?

Quite apart from the ethics of respecting Matthew's confidence, there was a practical consideration. How would David react to discovering that Matthew had grassed him? He might take it amiss—he might take it very much amiss—and the two of them had to go on working together. It was now April, and they were contracted until September. All evening every evening except Sunday, and all afternoon as well on Saturday, if the business held up, they had to occupy the stage together, reenacting the old friendship of Bohr and Heisenberg, reliving the old father-son relationship, reanimating the old conflicts and reconciliations. It was hard enough even if they were on the best of terms. I didn't want to make it any harder.

On the other hand, I couldn't *not* tell him. It wasn't possible for me to pretend to go on taking the thing seriously. Nor, in common humanity, could I let him go on laboriously forging away to no purpose.

Michael Blakemore and I phoned each other back and forth, working our way through the moral and practical complexities of the situation. One way or another, we decided, we should have to lure David into stepping out of his role as Mrs. Rhys-Evans, and into taking a bow in propria persona. Or, if we couldn't lure him, then perhaps we could panic him into it. Either way would no doubt involve his making rather a fool of himself, which was unfortunate. Not perhaps all *that* unfortunate, though, it seemed to us, in the circumstances.

There was a third possibility: to do both—to lure him *and* to panic him. A ghost of an idea began to take shape, like the first suggestion of a play or a novel coming on.

To carry it out I should need one or two unfamiliar faces and unfamiliar addresses. I enlisted the help of my children and stepchildren, and read them selected passages from the documents and correspondence to explain the case to them. Daughters and stepdaughters alike—sons-in-law and grandchildren, for that matter—all had the same reaction. They laughed and laughed. "Michael!" they gasped. "Dad! You didn't *really* believe any of this, did you?"

A serious question. Had I *really* believed it?

I'm not quite sure. I hadn't *not* believed it. Does one go around *believing* all the various bits of information that cross one's path in life? Not in any very active sense, surely. The question doesn't arise; it doesn't usually occur to one to examine things in that light. If you look at a list of train times to Manchester, it's not like being a conscientious young candidate for holy orders faced with the Thirty-nine Articles. You don't have to examine your soul and wrestle with doubt. If the timetable says that's when the trains arrive, that's when they arrive.

Yes, I had simply accepted it, in the way that one accepts the times of trains and almost everything else in life.

It was all very well for my children to laugh; they now had the benefit of hindsight. But would they really have laughed if I had read the text out to them before we'd all known the truth? Everyone had believed it, or seemed to, when I'd told them the story earlier! All they'd laughed at had been the funny bits—particularly the account of everyone crying over the death of Little Nell. My wife had read it out to her father, a scholar well used to taking a critical view, and he'd laughed like everyone else.

My daughters now—*now!*—claimed that they had discussed the documents among themselves and decided privately that they were a hoax. Only with some of the very youngest grandchildren and stepgrandchildren did respect for my sagacity remain intact.

Anyway, I set to work. First of all I wrote to Mrs. Rhys-Evans again, expressing contrition for my somewhat skeptical and perhaps rather over-hasty reaction to the anachronistic fragment of "Russian." I explained my theory about Farm Hall reverting to Intelligence purposes after the war, and suggested that the possibility of some later Russian involvement opened up intriguing possibilities—one of them being that the papers the family had discovered might become much more interesting to a publisher. I had discreetly sent an outline of the story, I said, to an old friend of mine who had contacts inside the Intelligence community, to see if he thought there might be anything in this.

The letter seemed to me to be remarkably temperate, courteous, and helpful, given the circumstances. Its only possible shortcoming was that it wasn't true. But you can't have everything.

It crossed with one from Mrs. Rhys-Evans, also expressing contrition. Her son, she said, had now confessed that the scrap of "Russian" was bogus—that he had written it himself in revenge for all my "legalistic tripe." It was too late, however, for me to avert the disastrous consequences of my fictitious helpfulness, undertaken with the best of fictitious motives, in showing the material to my fictitious friend with the fictitious connections in Intelligence. Five days later I had to write to Mrs. Rhys-Evans again in considerable haste, and in even more considerable embarrassment.

I had had a rather startling call, I told her, from some

idiot in the Ministry of Defence saying that he had reason
to believe I had various unauthorized documents in my possession, and ordering me to return them under threat of all
kinds of amazing and implausible penalties. I'd been so taken
aback that I hadn't been able to think what to say. Reflecting
on it afterward, though, I said, I supposed that my Intelligence connection—whose name, Mark, I now inadvertently
let slip—must have talked to someone.

> I told him not to worry about the Russian one because
> it was a forgery, but this seemed to make him more
> suspicious rather than less. He demanded to know who
> had sent me the documents. I refused to tell him, and
> I'm certain (fairly certain) I didn't send Mark copies of
> any of your covering letters, so they won't come ham-
> mering on *your* door, but I don't quite know what to
> do with the originals. If I give them up they'll presum-
> ably vanish into the same black hole that the Farm Hall
> transcripts were in for so long, and neither of us will
> ever see them again.

I asked her if I should send them back to her for safe-
keeping, and if all the rest of the documents, as I assumed,
were still safely with her son in France.

> If anyone does somehow start asking questions it
> would perhaps be sensible not to say anything about
> your suggestion of money changing hands, which
> might make the whole business sound less innocent
> than in fact it was.

All things considered, the letter was remarkably calm and collected, and full of sensible advice—not the kind of panic-stricken reaction that might have made Mrs. Rhys-Evans panic in her turn. After all, there was no real cause for panic. Yet. The only defect of the letter that I could see as I read it over was that, once again, it wasn't true.

But then it's difficult, as my man Martin Clay finds to his cost in my novel, not to get corrupted by the company you keep.

DB:

My first hint that something had changed came when I received an early-morning call from Celia—the real Celia. She sounded less than ever like her ficitious counterpart. Her voice was tight and panicky.

"David! I've had a letter from the Ministry of Defence! It's not very nice. They're saying I could go to prison!"

"Calm down, Cissy," I told her. "Just read it to me."

"It says 'Confidential. Dear Sir/Madam . . .' "

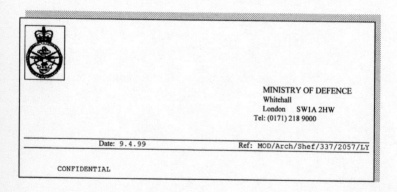

MINISTRY OF DEFENCE
Whitehall
London   SW1A 2HW
Tel: (0171) 218 9000

Date: 9.4.99   Ref: MOD/Arch/Shef/337/2057/LY

CONFIDENTIAL

"Which department is it from?"

"Whitehall. An assistant security officer."

Dear Sir/Madam . . . Following information received, it has come to my notice that you may be in possession of documents removed without authorisation from former MOD property. I am directed to require you to surrender any documents that you believe may fall within this category within seven days of the receipt of this letter. Failure to do so may expose you to the possibility of prosecution.

"It says I've got to send them Recorded Delivery to their office in Sheffield. And it says," she continued:

I must remind you that it is an offence under the Official Secrets Act 1989, punishable by a maximum of three months' imprisonment, or a fine up to level 5 (£2,500), to fail to comply with an official direction for the return or disposal of a document covered by the Act. Alternatively, proceedings may be instituted against you under civil law for breach of confidence, and an injunction sought for the return of the documents.

I must also remind you that disclosing a document protected against disclosure, while knowing or having reasonable cause to believe that it is protected against disclosure, is an offence punishable by a maximum of two years' imprisonment, and/or an unlimited fine.

"David, what am I going to do?"

I should like to give Michael the satisfaction of saying that this letter put the fear of God into me. I really would—now that we are both on this side of the keyboard. And if I couldn't honestly say that, then I should like to console him with the thought that at the very least I had a queasy moment. But I must be honest. I knew it was a hoax from the moment Celia began to read it out. Celia herself, I concede him this, was shaken—and wasn't entirely convinced by my reassurances; some days later she leapt to the conclusion that a man she found lurking up a telegraph pole outside her house was not a British Telecom engineer but a spy from the MOD.

But I knew from the first moment that it was a hoax because I was expecting something like this. I had always known that sooner or later the penny would drop. Sooner or later the sheer height of the heap of improbability that I had been piling up with a mechanical digger ever since the whole business began would bring it tumbling down to overwhelm Michael's determination to believe and his cunning in finding reasons to justify his belief. There are limits to the gullibility of even the cleverest of men!

Then again, as a hoaxer myself I am constantly on my guard. Ever watchful. Paul Scofield caught me out once, in retaliation for my little sally as Sgt. Blenkinsop of the Railway Police. So did another actor, Michael Simpkin, after an unfortunate episode in which he had managed to believe that I was a leading actress he had once worked with. We were in the living room of his house in Cricklewood when we suddenly heard . . . the muezzin, calling the faithful to prayer. At least *I* heard it, loud and clear—but Simpkin couldn't hear anything. Had he gone stone-deaf? Evidently not—he could hear *me,* and my growing bewilderment and alarm. He just couldn't hear the muezzin, and he watched me with a growing bewilderment and alarm of his own, until I began to think, So this is how it happens! This is how you can go mad. Not gradually, but suddenly, just like that! Out of nowhere, out of thin air—just like this hallucinatory muezzin.

Except, I realized, that it wasn't coming out of thin air . . . It was coming out of Simpkin's word processor!

Or, rather, out of the tape recorder that he had hidden beneath it.

Strange—these things aren't so funny when you're on the receiving end.

But the muezzin from the MOD didn't cause me a moment's anguish. Celia, too, I'm pleased to say, saw through it at once. *My* Celia, I mean, the fictitious one. She may not have been as clever as Frayn, but she had long experience in dealing with the dreadful Micheal's japes and wheezes, and when she sat down to reply she knew exactly what she was dealing with and who was responsible.

MF:

"I should tell you," wrote Mrs. Rhys-Evans, "that I have received another tiresome practical joke from my son Micheal, this time directed at me. It's an official-looking letter, supposedly from the MOD, threatening me with prison over the Farm Hall papers. He denies it of course, but it has his grubby fingerprints all over it: clumsy, obvious, badly researched, over the top."

The address of the Director, Archives, in Sheffield, she claimed, was known to every taxi driver to be the home of a lady of easy virtue, and she had discovered, from the billets-doux she had once been accustomed to receiving at one stage of her life from her boyfriend Kim Philby, that government departments always used 100 gsm paper, not 80 gsm.

So my first barrel had gone wide. Far from avenging my humiliation, it had opened me to more. My only consolation was that it had taken David five days to respond, and that the terms in which he denounced the forgery seemed to me

somewhat disproportionate. Maybe, privately, unacknow-
ledged, he *had* had a bad moment or two. . . .

In any case, as I had labored with computer and scanner
to capture the MOD logo off a letter I had received from
their library during my research for the play, and the OHMS
blazon and OFFICIAL PAID stamp off an old envelope from
Inland Revenue, I had been able to gain a little insight into
my tormentor's delight in forgery. Forgery, I had discovered,
is a very slow and fiddly business, but a curiously satisfying
one. It offers all the opportunities of fiction, together with
a clear and definite goal. In fact it had become an entertain-
ment for the whole family, with my elder stepdaughter sup-
plying the address of the Director, Archives, and my elder
son-in-law the authorship of the signature, while my
younger son-in-law posed as a neighbor to whom the letter
had been delivered in error and dropped it through Mrs.
Rhys-Evans's letter box for me, in order to save me from
the possibility of prosecution for passing OFFICIAL PAID mail
through the post.

Now what? I'd still failed to flush David Burke out. I had
another look at Mrs. Rhys-Evans's latest letter. "When I
write to you," she said, "I always look at that picture of
yours. I believe General Montgomery did this when he was
fighting Rommel in the desert: had his picture (not yours)
on the wall of his tent in Tobruk. It helped him get into
the mind of his adversary." She (he) was presumably referring to the photographs of the cast and production team in
the program. I got the program out of the file and looked
at the various pictures of David.

There he was in character as Niels Bohr, arguing with

Heisenberg: open, innocent, straightforward. And there he was as himself, gazing back at me, half-concealed behind a beard for some reason, his head turned mockingly a little to one side. He was smiling, but there was something a little unsettling about the smile. Sometimes you know that people are smiling insincerely, and it's because they are smiling with their mouth but not with their eyes. I covered up David's mouth and looked at his eyes. They were quite unmistakably smiling. His smile was sincere. Then for some reason I tried covering up the eyes and looking at the mouth. . . . It was the *mouth* that wasn't smiling.

I suddenly had the impression that I had a rather tough nut to deal with. Someone who was elusive rather than guileless, and remarkably obstinate. I in my turn felt a little like Rommel, gazing at a picture of Montgomery. An unfortunate position to find myself maneuvered into, of course, when you think of the outcome of the North African campaign.

Well, if I couldn't panic David, perhaps I could apply a little pressure on the character he was playing. Not Niels Bohr—Celia Rhys-Evans. If she was real. I rang up the Electoral Register Department at Hounslow Council; she was as real as Bohr. I should have liked to study *her* photograph a little. My helpful younger son-in-law, Oliver Wilson, who has long experience of making the kind of television programs that involve undercover operations against various kinds of suspected malefactors, offered to find out everything about her, including her ex-directory phone number, within half an hour. I nervously declined. He was a director with the Roger Cook investigative program at the time, and generously suggested that he should ask the large and terrifying Mr. Cook to doorstep her. I was tempted, I have to admit . . . but declined once again, and instead turned up unannounced myself with my wife for a friendly chat about the poor woman's problems with her semidelinquent son, and perhaps her recollections of Farm Hall, Kim Philby, and other matters. She was out. Just as well, possibly; however embarrassing she might have found the conversation, I should almost certainly have found it more embarrassing still. I'm no actor.

I explained all this to my daughter Susanna, back from BBC America in Washington for a few days. It inspired her to an ingenious piece of lateral thinking. I might not *be* an actor, she pointed out, but I *knew* one—a very fine one, who was particularly good at appearing guileless and innocent while at the same time being evidently extremely successful at hoaxing people. Why didn't I go to David Burke, she said, and explain to him that I now suspected that Mrs. Rhys-Evans was merely acting as the creature of a mysterious operator in the background? Then I could ask him to try and find out who it was by confronting her in some devious but guileless-seeming way while I looked on. He would surely feel, given the circumstances, that he owed me a favor. Though in all probability he would have to own up as soon as I put the idea to him. And if he actually had the cheek to take the job on, he would scarcely be able to carry it off without the truth emerging.

I took another look at David's photograph. He *might* have the cheek to take it on, it seemed to me. He might even manage to carry it off, just as he had carried off everything else so far. In which case the great tangle of fiction that we had all got ourselves enmeshed in would get into still worse knots.

A week later, I had to accompany a party of people to see the show, and I was still turning Susanna's idea over when I went round for the traditional call on the dressing rooms afterward. I had the impression that at the sudden sight of me David's famous guilelessness flickered a little. Was it my imagination, or did he look, just for a moment, a little shifty?

Looking shifty, it seemed to me, was the least he could do. Particularly since by this time he was negotiating behind my back with a friend of mine to make an even bigger fool of me.

Or so I hoped.

DB:

The latest recruit to our growing cast of characters believed firmly enough in his own existence, to judge from the size of his name in his letterhead:

Jürgen
Hoechst

- presse - fernsehen - funk -

//////// Haus Pegler, 81645 München, Athener Platz 8

Mrs. C. Rhys-Evans

He was a friend of Michael Frayn's, he said. Frayn had apparently given him the task of reading various German texts for him when he was researching *Copenhagen,* and had now asked him, while he was in London recently, to look at the documents Frayn had been sent by Mrs. Rhys-Evans. His command of English left a little to be desired, but he seemed to have his head screwed rather more firmly to his shoulders than poor Frayn. He confessed that he had found the documents very puzzling.

> I could not understand much more than Michael himself some of the pages. I left him on tenderhooks to know what he may find if you should persuade your son to let out more of these documents. But I must tell you privately that I for my part smelled a rat.
>
> I brought copies of these documents back to Munich, and I have made a little research of my own. According to one of documents, "O" should celebrate his birthday in Farm Hall. Now, who is "O"? I find that the only "O" at Farm Hall was Otto Hahn. I also find that the scientists were kept in Farm Hall from July 1945 until January 1946—and unfortunately Professor Hahn's birthday was in March.

So he suspected that something fishy was going on—a hoax on Frayn, in fact.

> I wonder if "C. Rhys-Evans" should be also perhaps a friend of Michael. Yes? My first guess is of course a rival dramatist. Do I detect by any chance the hand of Tom Stoppard behind this?

I was, of course, flattered to be identified with Stoppard. Particularly since Jürgen Hoechst had not Hoechst me for a moment, any more than the MOD had. Did Frayn really think I might be Tom Stoppard? Or was he still trying to flush me out? Was he hoping that vanity would make me boast "No! Not Tom Stoppard! Me—David Burke!" Because even though he had seen through Celia Rhys-Evans and her German documents, he still hadn't discovered who was behind them. Had he?

In any case I was not yet ready to yield to the proffered handcuffs. I was enjoying the writing too much.

I'll tell you something, Frayn, now that the whole thing's over: it was writing all those letters and documents that kept me going during the run of *Copenhagen*. It's a wonderful play, but it was so tiring to do! For all three of us. We'd take it in turns to come into the theatre looking like zombies. Never mind the play—the sheer number of stairs between the stage and the dressing rooms at the Duchess was a marathon in itself. Every night I counted them: 8 stairs down and 48 up from the stage door to the dressing room when I arrived in the evening, 56 stairs down to the stage at "Beginners." Same again up at the end of Act One; down at the beginning of Act Two; up again at the end of the play; 48 down and 8 up again to go home. That's 336 steps a night. We did 211 performances at the Duchess. That's 70,896 steps!

What I want to say, Michael, is that what kept me going through all those steps, days, weeks, months, was, yes—your play, of course—certainly—the play—but also that crazy gang of shadow figures that I was sharing with you. Writing! There's nothing like it! Well, you would know! You sit down in a corner. By yourself. With a sheet of paper and an old ballpoint. And out it comes! While the world, and all the steps in it, can go hang!

Of course, it's often rubbish. Tedious, boring, over the top. But then you hit your stride for a few yards, and you feel wonderful! You find a phrase that exactly expresses what you want to say about something. You read it back to yourself again and again. It feels good. You read it again the next day; it still feels good.

And perhaps you didn't want the performance to stop, either—your good friend Jürgen said he didn't expect me to drop my mask. "Rhys-Evans" I was and would remain. And he had a bone to pick with Frayn over his work on *Copenhagen*.

> I have to say frankly that I was a tiny bit angry to find no remark of all my help to Michael, neither in the theatre programme nor in the printed book, and I should be glad to get a little comeback at him.

So he had "a little proposal" to make.

> If you might continue the game, until you should have a good collection of these "documents," and also letters from Michael with his interesting responses to them, I believe you might get a rather nice book. Well, of course, if I am right about "Mrs C Rhys-Evans" she doesn't need an introduction to a British publishing house, but I think I might be helpful to publish this book in Germany. I can more or less promise you that it would find a good response here. We are a little sensible to the accusation that we have no sense of humour, and the sight of Werner Heisenberg, not to say "O," so to speak "getting his own back" from beyond the grave upon a British humour-writer would certainly be rather satisfying.

He listed his connections with German publishing houses and TV companies, and also offered to help Frayn translate any further documents I sent, "when perhaps I should be able to find all kinds of strange hidden meanings which should make him continue to be excited." He concluded:

In Germany we say: "Wer zuletzt lacht, lacht am besten." This I will leave your present collaborator to translate for you!

Thank you, Jürgen. In England, too, you may like to know, we say "He who laughs last . . ." I wrote back. I wasn't Tom Stoppard, I said, and I wasn't interested in the publishing venture Jürgen had suggested. "If this business is a hoax," I told him, "then someone else is doing the hoaxing. . . . My son, Micheal, is the likeliest candidate."

And I enclosed a long new chapter from my novel, in which Hans visited Stonehenge, where he realized that it was a prehistoric attempt to record the workings of the atom, and made friends with a German shepherd dog called Fritz. I introduced some excellent jokes (I thought) into the German manuscript. Well, Petra laughed.

I so much didn't want to stop writing! And Frayn didn't want to stop reading. Did he? This *was* what he meant? Wasn't it?

MF:

"*Wer zuletzt lacht* is, at this moment, me," my wonderful German agent, Ursula Pegler, had written when I sent her a copy of my treacherous friend's letter and asked her permission to adopt the address of her office as Jürgen's. Now she forwarded Mrs. Rhys-Evans's reply to him.

I read it hopefully. Hope faded. I seemed to be the only one in this relationship who could work up any normally respectable level of gullibility.

Well, at least Jürgen had raised a reply, which was more than the MOD had managed. It seemed unlikely, though, that David had any real belief in the poor fictitious creature's existence—particularly since Mrs. Rhys-Evans had also written to me to tell me about his proposal.

On the other hand, Mrs. Rhys-Evans went on to tell Jürgen that she *would* be interested in the publication of her novel, *Mystery at Farm Hall,* and in both her letter to him and her letter to me she enclosed a further installment of it. I found this puzzling. Did it suggest that David had some slight, provisional belief? Or that his creature, Celia Rhys-Evans, did on his behalf? Or that he was covering himself in case Jürgen actually existed, like an atheist offering up a furtive prayer?

Or did it mean that he was *pretending* to believe, in the hope that I would believe he believed, and would scale fresh heights of credulity?

In which case why was he pretending only to half-believe, or only half-pretending to believe, whichever it was? Why didn't he go the whole hog and offer to cooperate fully with Jürgen so as to draw me in? Was he covering himself against any possible accusation of *appearing* to believe, as the atheist might be careful to dissociate himself from his prayer by saying it in an ironic tone of voice?

Or was he simply suspending disbelief, like a spectator at a play, in order to allow the play to continue?

It was like a game of chess. Our initial strategies had both gone astray. Now I was counterattacking, and he was on the defensive. . . . Wasn't he? But how? What kind of position was he trying to develop?

I looked at the letters again. What struck me this time were the installments from *Mystery at Farm Hall*—not the content of them, but the fact that they had now expanded to cover five closely typed pages. This was surely a rather heavy investment of effort in a spoof. Particularly since David now knew, from the MOD letter if not from Jürgen's contribution, that the hoax was blown. The story seemed to be taking on a life of its own, quite independent of my belief or disbelief.

He *did* know the game was up, didn't he? I tried to put

myself in his place. He knew already, from the MOD letter, that I knew that the "documents" were a joke. He now knew, if he had seen through Jürgen, that I knew that the Mrs. Rhys-Evans of the covering letters was also a joke. So why did he carry on writing letters in her persona? Presumably becase he *didn't* know that I knew who it was who was actually writing them. . . . Or was *Mystery at Farm Hall* not the only story that was taking on a life of its own? Did the entire structure of deception now have some kind of enduring hold over both of us, as if the pages of a novel had opened to swallow us, or as if we had been sucked out of the darkness of the auditorium and absorbed into the action onstage?

Perhaps much the same confusion and alarm was beginning to seize David as well. "Where will all this end?" asked Mrs. Rhys-Evans plaintively in her letter to me. "I am beginning to wish that I'd never seen your play. I don't mean that unkindly. It's just that I am no longer young, and I feel as if I've fallen down a rabbit-hole."

A silence fell upon all of us. David was presumably waiting for some kind of response to his last few letters. But the MOD, after all their threats, took no further action, and Jürgen failed to follow up his ambiguous response from Mrs. Rhys-Evans. I didn't prompt either of them, or offer any further comment of my own. It was an unsatisfactory end to the story, but I simply couldn't think how to go on—or, to be honest, find the interest or energy to try. The thing would simply be left hanging, unresolved, like a late-night game of chess when both players finally become too exhausted and confused to continue.

Then, a month later, to my amazement, another letter arrived from Mrs. Rhys-Evans. "Here is the latest German bumph," she said. "Of course it is all Greek to me. I don't have anyone to translate it. I don't know any Germans personally, except Helmut Kohl. . . ." Enclosed was another laboriously handwritten installment of the journal, in which the author reported that he had been kept awake by terror after Major Rittner's reading of the murder of Nancy by Bill Sykes, and in which Heisenberg, unable to calculate the change from a two-shilling piece he had offered in the dining room for a cup of tea and a pancake costing one-and-sixpence, revealed that he couldn't do simple arithmetic. There was even a thumbnail sketch of Gerlach putting his hand up to ask a question, and making the author think that he was about to shout *"Sieg Heil!"*:

And another of Heisenberg playing them all the "Appassionata":

This was disconcerting enough. But then a few days later came a *second* letter, this time addressed to Jürgen Hoechst and forwarded by Ursula Pegler. "I am a little worried about Frayn," Mrs. Rhys-Evans told him. "I have not heard from him for several weeks." She mentioned the call I had reported getting from the MOD. "I do hope nothing unpleasant has happened to him. I've kept an eye on the obituary columns. I would be sad not to hear from him again. . . ."

And she enclosed yet another carefully crafted installment of the journal, in which the earlier mistake about the date of Otto Hahn's birthday was supposedly explained when he broke down and confessed that he had lied about it because he had felt so sad over the death of Little Nell and needed something to cheer himself up. Also enclosed, to both Jürgen and myself, were another five densely typed pages of *Mystery at Farm Hall.*

My heart sank under the weight of all this, and under the burden of my guilt for apparently failing to alert David to the fact that I now knew this was all a hoax, and leaving him to go blindly struggling on. But I *had* alerted him! Hadn't I? He had plainly understood the implications of the bogus MOD letter! So why *was* he going on? Who was fooling whom, and how? What in heaven's name was *happening*? I was completely lost. We seemed to be getting ever farther down the rabbit-hole. If this was chess, it was of the school known as "exotic"—a style developed, as I dimly recalled from my chess-playing days as a schoolboy, by the Soviet grandmaster Tal, who pursued strategies of such baffling complexity and opacity that his opponents couldn't begin to understand what he was trying to do.

I wondered whether I should have believed even these latest more baroque extravagances if Matthew hadn't rescued me. What—Helmut Kohl? Heisenberg's failure to solve the change equation? The explanation for the wrong date of Hahn's birthday? Surely I should have begun to balk by this time! Or perhaps I shouldn't have done. Though even *I* should have been stopped in my tracks by Major Rittner's joke about a German batman who failed to salute being "an insubordinate Klaus."

Oh, I don't know. I could probably have taken that in my stride like everything else.

I felt rather wistful in some ways for the irreversible loss of my innocence. I almost wished that I could un-know what I knew. I had enjoyed believing; I didn't enjoy not believing. The mystery had offered a hazy glow of indefinite promise; the solution to it contained nothing but embarrassment and dismay. Once, it seemed to me, I had sat on Father Christmas's knee in the twilit cardboard grotto and glimpsed the great treasure-house of delights to come; now

I could see that his beard was cotton wool and that he would be hanging his stocking up on Christmas Eve just like everybody else.

But what was I to do? How was I ever going to stop it? Perhaps even now David and his German scribe were working late and early on another stack of manuscript. Perhaps another kilogram of spoof fiction was winging its way to Munich. Perhaps the rest of our lives was going to be spent like this.

The summer solstice came and went. I had many other things on my mind. I did nothing.

DB:

Nothing. Nothing from Frayn, nothing from Jürgen. Nothing.

I felt as if one of my agents in the field had gone missing, nabbed by the enemy.

For a start, I thought Frayn must be away on holiday. But as the days became weeks and the weeks months, I realized that something else had happened. Petra and I would meet backstage at the Duchess. She would look at me expectantly, and I would shake my head sadly.

Where are you, Frayn? Why don't you answer? You can't leave me twisting in the wind! And it's not just me who's waiting! It's all of us: Celia and Micheal, and Celia's homeless husband, and the daughter who lives in Australia. You've left them all with nothing to do and nothing to say. And they've got so much that they want to tell you, if only you'd give them the chance!

Then there's the Germans: Heisenberg and Weizsäcker and poor crop-haired Gerlach. What about *them*, Frayn? Okay—I'll let Gerlach's hair grow and give him back his bow tie—if you can just allow him to exist! Aren't you curious about any of them? Don't you want to know why Heisenberg can't do simple arithmetic? Or why he always plays the "Appassionata" sonata? There are reasons for all these things. Serious reasons, funny reasons. But I can't tell you them unless you ask!

Am I feeling what Scheherazade would have felt if the old Sultan had died on her? Or worse, if he'd said, "Enough! Stop! No more! You can live! Just so long as I never have to listen to you saying 'Once upon a time' ever again!"

And then there's Hans! Poor little Hans! Scarcely more than a child, and his life's over already, almost before it had begun!

Are you feeling guilty, Frayn? You should be! Child-murderer!

Now come on, Burke, be reasonable. Who did I think I was? I was an actor who had played a joke on his writer. The writer had found out, and now he had more worthwhile things to get on with. But he had wanted to go on—he *had*—he'd told me in so many words! Or his creature had, on his behalf. "If you might continue the game," Jürgen had written, in his not-quite-perfect English, "until you should have a good collection of these 'documents,' . . . I believe you might get a rather nice book."

Language, or at any rate the written word, had once again let us down. A simple face-to-face conversation, complete with eye contact and body language, would have cleared the air in seconds. Why didn't he simply phone me and say: "Let's meet. I think we've got something to talk about"? For an obvious reason, now I came to think about it: because he didn't know who I was. All right, so why didn't I phone him? We could have had a glass of wine together. He could have blamed me for wasting his time. I could have said I was sorry. Had the conventions of the game taken over? Did they mean that all our transactions could be conducted only through fictitious intermediaries? Or had we come up against a certain natural reserve in both of us?

Whatever the reason, it was Shaw and Terry all over again. A certain strange intimacy had been achieved, and then it had been rudely broken off.

Eventually the penny dropped. Whatever he had wanted, as it seemed to me, he had clearly changed his mind. I felt wrong-footed. A genuine misunderstanding, no doubt, but I needed to dispel the uncertainty and banish any dark thoughts that might have ended our little dance together on a sour note.

A way had to be found to end things neatly. Somehow the runaway train had to be brought safely into the station, with both our egos still on the rails. I couldn't really expect Frayn to do it, any more than a burglar could expect the owner of the house he has broken into to show him out and wish him well.

We'd have to get Celia to help us. At the end of July, she took up her pen once again, as sadly this time as she had joyously before. It was the end of the affair.

MF:
Once again, at the sight of the familiar address and the familiar typescript, my spirits went down and my guilt was reawakened. I was wrong, though.

> Dear Michael, if I may call you that now?

I was touched by this new familiarity—particularly by the care she had taken to spell my name the same way as I did.

> It is sad, but I must bring this Farm Hall business to a close. I know you will be shattered, but it is simply taking up too much of my time. I am a writer now, thanks to you, and that must come first. One has a duty to one's public.

And, rather like a former lover demanding the return of her letters, she asked me to return the German manuscripts. Not to her Chiswick address, though, but c/o Burke, at a familiar-looking address in Kent.

She signed it Cissy, with three kisses. I blew Cissy many heartfelt kisses back—and I blew them c/o Burke. She had finally come up trumps, and rescued us both from the swamp just as elegantly and skillfully as she had dropped us into it in the first place.

I gratefully picked up my cue. I entirely understood, I said in my reply; we were perhaps getting to know each other a little too well, and if this thing had gone on we might not have been able to control our feelings indefinitely. I had noticed my wife looking at me a little oddly as I kept talking to her about Celia Rhys-Evans, and I imagined that Cissy, too, had had a few odd looks from her husband; which was no doubt why she had asked me to write to an accommodation address.

Curious, I said, that her understanding friend was called Burke, because I also knew someone of that name who lived in the same part of Kent. The one I knew, however, was an extremely guileless and sweet-natured individual, who was most unlikely to get mixed up in devious activities involving the passing on of clandestine packages.

Or perhaps, I suggested, it *was* the same one. Perhaps my Mr. Burke was rather more devious than I had realized. I had to see my one shortly, I told her, for the last night of the first cast of my play, so I should take her manuscripts to the restaurant with me afterward, and see if he blushed when he saw her name on the envelope.

DB:

So at the last-night dinner the two of us finally spoke face-to-face about it all, as I had looked forward to doing, and all things were made clear. With the brown envelope of papers on the floor between our chairs, we retraced the strange journey we had pursued together yet apart for the last few months.

We realized, as we talked about it, how often coincidence, accident, and even error had played a part in the story, as if someone or something out there was conspiring to make fools of both of us. Michael said that the detail that had convinced him beyond anything else that the German documents were genuine was the effortless native fluency of my double *s*. I said I didn't know what he was talking about. He wrote it on the tablecloth for me: β. I had to confess that I had never even known there *was* such a letter—I thought it was a capital *B*.

I told him about some of my earlier hoaxes, and said that I was coming to the conclusion that people would believe anything—that indeed they preferred to believe the unlikely.

Try founding a religion on the assertion that water will wet you and fire will burn you, and you will whistle in the wind. Tell them that water is really their great-grandmother come back to see them, and that fire can only heal them, and the queue of eager believers will stretch round the block.

I had after all warned Michael Blakemore in so many words that the papers must be a hoax, just as I had warned my earlier victims about the Lover of Hats and the woman who had recognized her family photographs. Once again my warning had been peremptorily brushed aside. Perhaps everyone's faith had even been reinforced by these challenges from an unbeliever.

So how had Frayn finally managed to see through it? He confessed that someone had squealed. He wouldn't say who, but it wasn't hard to guess. I looked at Matthew, sitting on the other side of Michael. "Was it you?" I asked. He nodded. Of course. He had after all pleaded with me to stop, to kick my addiction. I couldn't really feel angry with him. I didn't toss my drink in his face or even chide him. I knew he had done it out of kindness to Frayn. And how could I berate a man I had so enjoyed sharing a stage with?

I had ended Celia's last letter to Frayn "Yours uncertainly." It was not entirely facetious. Personal identity is a shifting thing. We all feel like different people at different times and with different companions: a king or queen at home, a serf at work. Or vice versa. It's doubly true of an actor, of course, who is professionally obliged to be different people. It's in his contract, and he can be sacked if he fails to change from David Burke to Niels Bohr or whoever it may be on the stroke of 7:30.

I usually have no problem about changing back again at

10:30. I'm happy to swap doublet and hose, or Bohr's good solid three-piece suit, for sweater and trousers when the curtain comes down. I like being a real person once more. But I have to confess I was a little sad to take my leave of Bohr for the last time. Not to mention Sara and Margrethe, and Matthew and Heisenberg. Or for that matter Celia and Micheal, Gerlach and Hans.

So when Frayn sprang his little surprise on me in return, and suggested writing something about our joint discovery of the missing documents, I agreed at once. It wasn't till I was on my way home that the full implication hit me. It was almost as if he had heard my plea not to let it all stop. The journey was to go on.

I'm aware that it may mean I shall henceforth be remembered only as a practical joker, and that when I walk into rehearsal rooms in the future I will be greeted by cries of "Here he comes! Watch out for the water pistol, lads! Where's the whoopee cushion?"

And my personality would change in everyone's eyes once again. My credit as an actor had already gone up simply by my having assumed the personality of a genius. Hitherto, casting directors had seen me as earthbound and middlebrow—a GP rather than a consultant, Redbrick rather than Oxbridge. Then suddenly I was a theoretical physicist. Now I was to take on yet another role, as a writer. I could imagine the irritation in the casting departments. "Doris! Refile David Burke with John Wood and Paul Rhys under Poets and Eccentrics. . . . I wish these actors wouldn't keep moving about. It doesn't make our job any easier."

Here's another coincidence. As I was writing these final sections of our book, I kept finding a particular sheet of printed paper endlessly in the way, as if it had a life of its own and was determined to insinuate itself into our narrative. When at last I took a closer look at it, I discovered that it was the opening page of a paper written by my brother, Liam Burke, who is a professor of physiology in Australia. He has had some serious trouble with one of his eyes, and with remarkable detachment decided to write up his own case for the journals. It occurred to me that this is what Frayn and I should be doing with the paper that *we* were going to write. We should be turning our private experience of another sort of defective vision into a useful case study for the enlightenment of the public.

Can the leopard change his spots quite so completely and quite so quickly, though? I'm tempted to play one last trick on you, Frayn, before the story's over. To pick up the phone and remind you of what we agreed over that last-night dinner: that if, when we had finished writing, either of us felt that we didn't want to let the manuscript see the light of day . . .

You'd believe it, too, wouldn't you, Michael?

Epilogue

MF:

One day that summer, at a guest night in my old Cambridge college, I sat next to someone who told me that Farm Hall was now occupied by Marcial Echenique, the professor of architecture at Cambridge, and his wife, Maria Louisa, a mathematican and computer expert. I was emboldened to do what I should have done much earlier, when I was re-searching the play, and wrote to the Echeniques asking if I might see the inside of the house. They at once, with great kindness, invited my wife and me to lunch.

So, on a perfect English summer's day, we drove up to Godmanchester. It is a classically pretty village, just across the old and narrow brick bridge over the Great Ouse from Huntingdon. And there, on the outskirts of the village, was Farm Hall—the real Farm Hall. It is a most beautiful eighteenth-century house, backed by enchanted walled gardens and great lawns that open out onto the woods and distances of the flat Fenland landscape.

Professor Echenique showed us over the house. He pointed out the discreet door leading to a separate wing that he believed must have housed the eight British eavesdroppers and their equipment, and explained how the elegant reception rooms on the piano nobile had once been partitioned to provide accommodation for the ten German scientists. Erich Bagge (the member of the German team who really *had* kept a diary) had paid a nostalgic return visit, said Professor Echenique. They had all enjoyed their stay in the house, Bagge had told him; so perhaps the lighthearted atmosphere of fun in the dorm that prevails in the spoof journal was not all that wide of the mark after all.

Bagge also had one darker memory. When the partitions had been in place, he told Professor Echenique, the central section of what is now the drawing room had been Otto Hahn's quarters. The published transcript for the terrible night when they all heard the news of Hiroshima records the fear Heisenberg and the others felt that Hahn, tormented by guilt for the part he had played in the development of the bomb by his discovery of fission, might attempt suicide. Bagge had pointed to the hook in the ceiling of the drawing room from which the chandelier is now suspended. Hahn, he said, had actually attempted to hang himself from it.

It was another detail of Professor Echenique's account, though, that struck a particular chord with me. When he and his wife had acquired the house, they had had no more inkling of its previous history than Mrs. Rhys-Evans had. Then one day they had discovered concealed false beams full of wiring with no apparent connection to any of the domestic lighting or power circuits—a mystery that had completely baffled them until one of the professor's students told him that he had been reading Robert Jungk's book about the development of the bomb, *Brighter than a Thousand Suns,* and had come across a strange reference to the house.

What struck me most of all were the circumstances in which Professor Echenique had discovered the hidden wiring, and had the first intimations of a buried past.

He had taken up the floorboards.

Life not imitating art, in this case, but prefiguring it.

Or did some passing shadow of newly learned suspicion cross my mind when Professor Echenique told me that?

Of course not. Not the faintest shadow. The earth was beginning to settle down beneath my feet again by this time. I was back to where I was the first time I heard of those same floorboards yawning open to reveal their curious secrets, back to believing whatever I was told, just as we all are.

More or less.